Race Literature

SUBSCRIPTION PRICE, $1.00 PER YEAR. SINGLE COPY, 25 CENTS.

Vol. 20, No. 3.   JANUARY, 1904.   Whole No. 79.

Women Contributors to the *A.M.E. Church Review*, 1884-1924

CYNTHIA LEE PATTERSON

University Press of Mississippi / Jackson

The University Press of Mississippi is the scholarly publishing agency of the Mississippi Institutions of Higher Learning: Alcorn State University, Delta State University, Jackson State University, Mississippi State University, Mississippi University for Women, Mississippi Valley State University, University of Mississippi, and University of Southern Mississippi.

www.upress.state.ms.us

The University Press of Mississippi is a member of the Association of University Presses.

Chapter 5 used with permission of University of Chicago Press— The Journal of African American History, from *"Notes of Travel" in the A.M.E. Church Review, 1903–1912: Precursor to the Green-Book, Feminized Sociology,* Association for the Study of African-American Life and History 106, no. 1 (2021): 52–77; permission conveyed through Copyright Clearance Center, Inc.

Publication of this book was supported in part by funding from the University of South Florida Provost's Office.

Copyright © 2026 by University Press of Mississippi
All rights reserved
Manufactured in the United States of America

∞

Publisher: University Press of Mississippi, Jackson, USA
Authorised GPSR Safety Representative: Easy Access System Europe - Mustamäe tee 50, 10621 Tallinn, Estonia, gpsr.requests@easproject.com

Library of Congress Cataloging-in-Publication Data

Names: Patterson, Cynthia Lee, author.
Title: Race literature : Women contributors to the A.M.E. Church Review, 1884–1924 / Cynthia Lee Patterson.
Description: Jackson : University Press of Mississippi, 2026. | Includes bibliographical references and index.
Identifiers: LCCN 2026004213 (print) | LCCN 2026004214 (ebook) | ISBN 9781496861689 (hardback) | ISBN 9781496861696 (trade paperback) | ISBN 9781496861702 (epub) | ISBN 9781496861719 (epub) | ISBN 9781496861726 (pdf) | ISBN 9781496861733 (pdf)
Subjects: LCSH: African Methodist Episcopal Church—Periodicals. | African Methodist Episcopal Church—History. | Race in literature. | Literature and race—United States. | African American women authors—United States—History and criticism. | Women authors, Black—United States—History and criticism. | American literature—African American authors—History and criticism.
Classification: LCC PS153.B53 P38 2026 (print) | LCC PS153.B53 (ebook)
LC record available at https://lccn.loc.gov/2026004213
LC ebook record available at https://lccn.loc.gov/2026004214

British Library Cataloging-in-Publication Data available

*For my ancestors, Alda and Helen;
and for my progeny, Hailey and Caitlin:
powerfully strong women, all.*

Contents

ACKNOWLEDGMENTS ix

INTRODUCTION 3

CHAPTER 1: Beyond "Creation and Transmission
of Literary Culture" 17

CHAPTER 2: AME Churchwomen Making History 40

CHAPTER 3: Sociological Writings: Home, Family, Church 53

CHAPTER 4: Sociological Writings: Suffrage, Temperance,
Criminality, Prison Reform 64

CHAPTER 5: E. Marie Carter's "Notes of Travel" Column,
1903–1912 87

CHAPTER 6: Matters Educational 114

CHAPTER 7: Matters Scientific and Philosophical 125

CONCLUSION: Writing Race Literature in Extraordinary Times . . . 142

APPENDIX: Women Contributors and Their Articles
in the *A.M.E. Church Review*, 1884–1924. 145

NOTES 151

INDEX 177

Acknowledgments

Many folks have aided me in bringing this project to fruition over the past ten-plus years. I began this project with the encouragement of Eric Gardner, the book editor for the journal *American Periodicals*, which I was coediting with Jean Lee Cole. Eric had just completed *Black Print Unbound* (2015) about the impact of *The Christian Recorder*, its editors, and its contributors—both men and women—on African American literature and culture during the Civil War period. I knew that since the founding of the *A.M.E. Church Review* in 1884, the publication had been an important space for the theological writings of the clergymen of the AME denomination, but I wondered what the church's female members—many of them the wives or daughters of AME clergy—had contributed to the quarterly during this later period A "church lady" myself, I knew that balancing the demands of church responsibilities with the demands of being a "writing woman" sometimes proved challenging. What sorts of challenges had confronted these earlier church ladies in their efforts to claim their own culture authority? I thank Eric for encouraging me to pursue these research questions.

Over the next two years, I spent my breaks from the University of South Florida conducting research in the archives of the Rembert E. Stokes Library at Ohio's Wilberforce University, near the town where I grew up, which holds a nearly complete print run of the *A.M.E. Church Review*. I heartily thank archivist Jacqueline Brown, who came out of retirement to assist with my project, and librarian Colin Dube, who granted me access to the bound volumes of the *Review*. Stephenie Rostron relocated the *Review* volumes from their precarious perch on the third floor beneath a leaky roof to what she identified as their original location on the second floor. Archivists Mackenzie Snare and Rachel Knight answered queries and provided high-resolution scans of several images from the *Review*. Wilberforce's former executive vice president and provost, Elfred Anthony Pinkard supported efforts to digitize the *Review*, though they have not yet come to fruition. Warren Watson and especially Lynn Ayers at the Reverdy C. Ransom Library at Payne Theological Seminary greatly assisted my research there.

The University of South Florida Humanities Institute provided a summer 2018 travel grant to visit the archives at Drew University, where I gathered more than a thousand scans from issues of the *Review* unavailable at Wilberforce and benefited greatly from the assistance of Candace Reilly, Brian Shetler, and Alex Parrish. Other archivists who answered queries over the years include Sonia Basnight (Hampton University), Kathy Shoemaker (Rose Library, Emory University), and Jordan Sprunger and Karis Blaker (Garrett Evangelical Theological Library). Special thanks go to Karis Blaker at Garrett, who provided two images that grace the cover and interior of this book.

An Andrew W. Mellon Residential Research Fellowship in African American History allowed me to spend a month in the summer of 2021 conducting research at the Library Company of Philadelphia, Historical Society of Pennsylvania, and Mother Bethel Archives in Philadelphia, where Margaret Jerrido was most helpful. At the Library Company, I thank Deirdre Cooper Owens, Jasmine Smith, Sarah Weatherwax, Emily Guthrie, Erika Piola, Fran Dolan, and especially Abigail Guidry, who provided high-resolution digital scans for eight of the figures featured in the book. At the Historical Society of Pennsylvania, I thank Sarah Helm and Christina Larocco.

Jennifer Ritterhouse, Michele Valerie Ronnick, and Andreá N. Williams read portions of chapters and provided feedback. Tangela

Serls at the University of South Florida invited me to participate in a panel discussion in which Saidiya Hartman talked about her book *Wayward Lives, Beautiful Experiments* that helped me realize that Saidiya's wayward ladies and my church ladies were one and the same. Other scholars who helped me refine the ideas in this project include Teresa Fry Brown, Dwain Coleman, Rita B. Dandridge, Christina Davidson, Christina M. Dickerson, Brigitte Fielder, Cheryl Fish, Janet Gray, Paul Harrison, Will Hogue, Antoinette T. Jackson, Mitch Katchum, April Logan, Joycelyn Moody, Elizabeth Renker, Kwabena Slaughter, Candacy Taylor, Dreamal Worthen, Nazera Wright, and Elissa Zellinger.

The members of my weekly writing group listened attentively to project updates and offered expert advice: Amy Blair, Donna Campbell, Melissa Homestead, and Debby Rosenthal. University of South Florida graduate research assistants Heather Fox and Janie Gill helped in the early stages of my research.

I received valuable feedback from AME Church members and clergy Oryan Speed (St. Paul AME, Apalachicola, Florida) and Alvin Jackson (St. James AME, New Orleans); the Reverend Dr. Rhella Murdaugh (Mt. Zion AME, Ocala, Florida). University Press of Mississippi editors Emily Bandy, Katie Turner, and Craig Gill shepherded this book into print. For any remaining errors, please accept my apology: I did the best I could, and it will be left to future scholars to correct any unintentional errors remaining.

Finally, I give special thanks to the church ladies (and gentlemen) of the Unitarian Universalist Church of St. Petersburg, Florida, where I have led a Sunday morning book discussion group for many years. This faith community remains an ongoing source of spiritual sustenance.

NOTE: Because archival records vary in the spelling of names and locations, this text follows the usage found in each primary source.

Race Literature

Introduction

The cover of the January 1901 issue of the *A.M.E. Church Review*, the quarterly publication of the African Methodist Episcopal (AME) denomination, boldly boasts, "TWENTIETH CENTURY NUMBER—ALL THE CONTRIBUTORS WOMEN."[1] The issue's table of contents spotlights prominent women active in Black public life at the turn of the century—Fanny Jackson Coppin, Katherine Davis Tillman, Josephine Silone Yates, Mary Church Terrell, and Gertrude Bustill Mossell— as well as some half-dozen other lesser-known AME churchwomen. In the issue's "Editorial Department" column, editor Hightower T. Kealing asserts, "For the first time in its life of seventeen years, the *Review* goes to its readers with all of its contributors women; and certainly for variety, vivacity, strength and fascinating interest, no other number excels it" (281). Kealing adds, "That such a galaxy of capable writers, representing, each one, some special line of useful activity among us, can be brought together in one number of a magazine standing for the highest in thought, the broadest in view and the chastest in form, is the most remarkable comment on race progress that can be made. Every article deserves close and critical perusal, and we are sure all the articles will repay it."

By the "highest in thought," Kealing was likely referencing the religious and theological contributions submitted to other issues primarily by the denomination's male clergy and geared toward the spiritual uplift of rank-and-file AME members and other readers, both Black and white. However, the quarterly also regularly published contributions from well-known Black male luminaries such as Frederick Douglass, Booker T. Washington, W. E. B. Du Bois, and T. Thomas Fortune. Although Kealing was neither the first nor the only editor of a religiously affiliated publication to boast about the journal's quality, he prioritized expanding the quarterly's offerings beyond AME denominational concerns. As Frances Smith Foster has pointed out, "The Afro-Protestant press rarely if ever confined itself to what we might understand as 'religious' subjects. To the publishers and contributors, as to their intended readers, the sacred and the secular were not discrete elements of their lives and their experiences."[2] Frank Luther Mott, the early historian of American periodicals, recognized the *Review* as a general-interest magazine, pronouncing it one of the most important Methodist periodicals founded by African Americans.[3] Kealing began his editorship in July 1896 by declaring "The Review is more than denominational; it is racial, national, it is cosmopolitan" (175). He promised that the quarterly would not limit itself to "discussions of the religious and theological questions"; rather, it would include matters "political, sociological, historical, archaeological, educational and philosophical" (175).

But Kealing failed to delineate exactly what constituted such matters. He likely was aware of Victoria Earle Matthews's July 30, 1895, address to the First Congress of Colored Women: under Kealing's predecessor, Levi J. Coppin, the *Review* had published four pieces by Matthews.[4] The congress, organized in response to journalist John Jacks's attack on Black women, brought together groups that would eventually unite to form the National Association of Colored Women. In her address, subsequently circulated in pamphlet form and titled "The Value of Race Literature," Matthews lays out the various forms that race literature might take: "History, Biographies, Scientific Treatises, Sermons, Addresses, Novels, Poems, Books of Travel, miscellaneous essays." Matthews goes on to present examples of race writers who have contributed to such genres. Not surprisingly, perhaps, she credits male writers for contributing history (William C. Nell), biography (Douglass), scientific (Nostrand), and philosophical writings (Professor R. T. Greener) while citing the contributions of "our veteran literary women" in the areas of "poetry, songs, and addresses." Matthews also credits Josephine St. Pierre Ruffin's *Woman's Era* with featuring the contributions of Black women writers. Concludes Matthews, "Woman's part in Race Literature, as in Race building, is the most important part, and has been so in all ages."[5]

Kealing seems to have agreed with Matthews's assessment of the importance of women's associational endeavors and intellectual work to racial uplift. In his October 1896 editorial, Kealing wrote, "the woman's association is the greatest race movement of the times," adding, "The time has come when women have use for their heads as well as their hearts" (237, 247). A sampling of the contents of the January 1901 issue demonstrates Kealing's commitment to featuring women's contributions to the broad categories Matthews had outlined as central to race literature: Tillman's "Heirs of Slavery, A Little Drama of To-Day" (199–203); Yates's "French Literature in the Seventeenth Century" (204–12); Terrell's "A Reply to a Statement Recently Made" (216–21); and Mossell's "The Afro-American Council from an Absentee's Point of View" (222–25).

Mossell's and Terrell's contributions served as harbingers of the "race progress" that Kealing touted in this issue. Mossell praised the progress of the recently held Afro-American Council in Indianapolis. Terrell, in her third and final contribution to the quarterly in this era, refuted the assertions made by Charles Dudley Warner shortly before his death about Black education.[6] Both Mossell and Terrell championed the significant progress made by African Americans in the forty years following emancipation. Following these featured articles were the quarterly's regular "departments" during Kealing's editorship: Women; Religious; Educational; Sociological; Scientific; Miscellaneous; and Editorial. The January 1901 special issue thus highlighted what race literature could look like from the pens of women contributors.

As the third editor and first layman to head the *Review*, Kealing brought to the journal an extensive background in education: he had served as principal at several Black educational institutions. Accordingly, he possessed fresh ideas for subject matter and a willingness to encourage women contributors to move beyond their previous writing in the realms of poetry, fiction, and drama. In his embrace of new genres, new topics, and increased contributions from women writers, Kealing proved ideally suited for the times in which he found himself, an age scholars have dubbed the Progressive Era, the Woman's Era, or the Postbellum, Pre-Harlem Era.[7]

This book focuses on women's contributions beyond the traditional literary genres of poetry, fiction, and drama, highlighting subject matter consistent with Matthews's and Kealing's vision for an expanding race literature. During his editorship, which lasted until 1912, Kealing explicitly encouraged authors to explore this wider range of material, and not just Black male clergy but also women writers increasingly embraced these new subjects during the Progressive Era, contributing reportage and travel writing as well as essays on education, science, philosophy, history, and sociology.

Although nominally a denominational organ, the *A.M.E. Church Review* was conceived as a general-interest magazine for the race. Though the AME was not the largest Black denomination in this era—its 494,777 members in 1906 amounted to less than a quarter of the number of Black Baptists, for example—the *Review* continues to publish in the twenty-first century and has thus outlasted many of Baptist periodicals that began publishing in the late nineteenth century, among them *The National Baptist Magazine*, which ran from 1894 to 1901 and, like the *Review*, featured primarily contributions from men but included women's contributions as well.[8]

Much important scholarship has emerged in recent years on African American periodicals, including Eric Gardner's 2015 book *Black Print Unbound* (on *The Christian Recorder*) and Benjamin Fagan's 2016 book *The Black Newspaper and the Chosen Nation* (on *The Colored American*). In addition, two recent edited collections sketch out the contours of Black women's intellectual history in the United States, including their contributions to periodicals.[9] However, women's contributions to religious publications remain underexplored perhaps largely because of issues relating to the preservation of and access to denominational publications.[10] For example, according to WorldCat, the full run of the *A.M.E. Church Review* is available in print only at Wilberforce University and on microfilm at a few other libraries. Only a couple of dozen issues from this era are available digitally.[11]

Even when religiously affiliated writings of Black women prove available via periodicals or elsewhere, scholarly reticence may persist except among those working broadly on the history of religion. As Joycelyn Moody suggests in her work on Black holy women's spiritual autobiographies, "African American feminist scholars" may still have a "vexed relationship" with the "stereotype of the black church woman."[12] Though Moody wrote these words at the turn of the twenty-first century, they likely remained true over the ensuing years. Thus, some scholars of Black history and culture may have avoided the writings of churchwomen, especially when focused on matters of the Christian faith and practice.

Yet as literary scholar Andreá N. Williams and others have noted, African American periodicals—including religious periodicals—frequently served as the only venues in which Black women writers could place their work.[13] And while some scholarly attention has been paid to the better-known women authors who contributed primarily poetry, fiction, and drama to the *A.M.E. Church Review*—Frances Ellen Watkins Harper, Alice Dunbar Nelson, and Tillman, for example—scant scholarship focuses on the hundreds of contributions from rank-and-file AME Church members or on nonliterary genres.[14] This book works to fill in some of these gaps, functioning largely as a recovery effort while contributing to the ongoing scholarship in Black periodical studies, the Afro-Protestant press, Black women's intellectual history, Black travel writing, and the prehistory of sociology and offering new biobibliographical research on lesser-known women writers.[15]

So who were the women who contributed race literature to the *A.M.E. Church Review* between 1884 and 1924? As in the case of the January 1901 issue, many were prominent educators and writers already recognized for their contributions both to the burgeoning women's club movement and to the Black press. But the journal also featured a host of lesser-known writers and educators, most with ties to women's clubs. As scholar Brittney C. Cooper points out, the nationalization of the club movement allowed Black women to address a much larger "race public opinion" audience.[16] And the *Review* also printed pieces by dozens of AME churchwomen—many the wives of clergymen and church leaders—and by a handful of white women sociologists and activists.

Most of the these contributors appear to have hailed from what Williams identifies as the "middle class" or the "better class," and some specifically addressed class issues. However, some of the rank-and-file AME churchwomen likely hailed from more humble origins but had obtained education and become professional teachers or social service providers—operating orphanages, working in prison reform, running Sunday schools—or volunteered with churches, women's clubs, and other community social institutions. Moreover, while most women contributors rehearse a rhetoric of racial uplift, some of their submissions betray what Williams identifies as "class anxiety," particularly an awareness of "class disparities" and fears that the actions of some of their less fortunate sisters might reverberate to the disgrace of the entire race.[17]

Women contributors also weighed in on issues of race, gender, and sex. Historian Mia Bay notes that antebellum women writers rarely engaged in intellectual debates involving the relative merits of the individual races.[18] A few of these authors specifically referenced issues of comparative racial thought in essays on race history and sociological concerns. Gender issues were generally addressed in the "Women" column and took the form of summaries of or excerpts from articles published in other periodicals. Titles such as "Dimensions of a Perfect Woman" (July 1903) and "It Takes a Woman to Make a Home" (October 1900) exemplify this material, which might be labeled conservative by today's standards. Kealing identified the sources of these articles but usually provided no information about the author's gender. However, women contributors to the *Review* did treat issues of gender and sex.

The AME Church's dedication to print media dates back to Bishop Richard Allen's 1816 election and establishment of the AME Book Concern. Early on, the book concern published primarily conference meeting minutes, the denomination discipline doctrine, and hymnals. In 1841 the denomination inaugurated *The AME Church Magazine*, based in Brooklyn, New York, to replace the various conference publications. Although intended as a monthly, *The AME Church Magazine* published "quite irregularly," largely because readers could not afford to subscribe. *The AME Church Magazine* resembled a literary periodical, soliciting contributions from "especially those who chose to write poetry or essays on religious topics."[19]

In 1848 the denomination launched a weekly newspaper, *The Christian Herald*, renamed *The Christian Recorder* in 1852. The *Recorder* originally contained material similar to that of as the *Magazine*. However, as Gardner points out, the *Recorder* also published features typically found in newspapers rather than literary magazines—obituaries, marriage notices, letters from readers, and advertisements seeking information about long-lost relatives.[20]

In 1858, under the direction of Bishop Daniel Payne, the AME Church launched an Indianapolis-based literary periodical, *The Repository of Religion and Literature and of Science and Art*. Intended as a quarterly that would replace the various "literary societies organized within the district conferences," the publication subsequently moved to Philadelphia and then to Baltimore. The *Repository* solicited contributions from both established and unknown writers and like the nonsectarian literary periodicals of the day featured engraved portraits by John Sartain, the era's leading mezzotint

Figure 0.1. Benjamin T. Tanner. Courtesy the Library Company of Philadelphia Reading Room.

engraver. Like the *Magazine*, the *Repository* suffered from financial instability and was "temporarily suspended for almost a year" before ceasing publication entirely in April 1864.[21]

The first issue of the *Review* appeared in July 1884, with subsequent issues published every July, October, January, and April. While male authors contributed the vast majority of the contents, the first editor, the Reverend Benjamin T. Tanner (1884–88), also solicited contributions from women writers, relying on his previous experience editing *The Christian Recorder*.[22] Editors were initially appointed for a four-year stint but could receive reappointment. Tanner was succeeded by Levi J. Coppin (1888–96), Kealing (1896–1912), and Reverdy C. Ransom (1912–24).

In the early years of publication, the *Review* tended to treat mostly the religious concerns of the denomination, with ministers, bishops, and male educators contributing articles on doctrine, church discipline, missionary endeavors, and the like while women writers contributed poetry and short and serial fiction. Tanner and

FIGURE 0.2. LEVI J. COPPIN. COURTESY THE LIBRARY COMPANY OF PHILADELPHIA READING ROOM.

FIGURE 0.3. HIGHTOWER T. KEALING. COURTESY THE LIBRARY COMPANY OF PHILADELPHIA READING ROOM.

Coppin were ordained ministers prior to editing the quarterly, so their preference for such topics is not surprising. Kealing, in contrast, was the first layman to serve as editor and had served as principal at several Black educational institutions. Accordingly, he brought in fresh ideas and announced his intention to expand the scope of material published in the quarterly and to limit its articles to "fresh matter prepared especially for the Review" (July 1896, 175).

This widened scope opened the door for women contributors to demonstrate their mastery of other genres. According to David W. Wills, between 1884 and 1889, only 14 percent of the matter in the journal was contributed by women, a low rate that he contends implies that "women were to be centrally involved in the creation and transmission of literary culture, but not in the discussion of major public questions—including that of their own role."[23] However, a closer examination of Coppin's tenure reveals that 20 percent of the matter contributed to the quarterly during that time was attributed to women.[24] As historian Derrick Spires notes, Black authors commonly used pseudonyms during this period.[25] Yates contributed a half dozen lengthy essays under an ambiguous pseudonym (R. K. Potter), and other women may also have done so, a phenomenon that may have affected Wills's calculations.[26]

Cooper points out that dismissals of Black women's contributions to public culture predate Wills by at least three-quarters of a century: in an 1899 article, W. E. B. Du Bois declared a recent meeting of the largely male National Afro-American Council "more relevant to the concerns of the race as a whole" than a contemporaneous convention of the National Association of Colored Women. Cooper finds Du Bois's "crude characterization" of the women's group "rooted in a politics of racial manhood" that sought to "confine Black women's participation to work traditionally understood as feminine and therefore intellectually unserious."[27] Though women's contributions may have been overlooked, they could and did contribute to major public questions in this era. And by writing in his October 1898 editorial that writers would be "admitted solely on merit. No one is excluded who has an important message well delivered and opportunely sent" (656), Kealing was explicitly welcoming contributions from women.

My analysis excludes most women-authored reports on missionary societies as well as letters from women who were responding to *Review* articles about religious practices—for example Edna C. Thomas's article answering an earlier query, "What Is Good Preaching?" (October 1903, 110–11). I selected material representing a wide range of views but limited my analysis primarily to better-known authors and lesser-known writers for whom I could compile at least a meager biobibliographical background portrait. Consequently, I examine more than four dozen women writers who contributed about fifty articles between 1884 and 1924. Most of these authors and writings have received scant scholarly attention.

The challenges of a project of this nature include both the broad chronological sweep and the many and varied voices of the women contributors. No single thread links all the contributions. Instead these women writers assumed a variety of rhetorical positions in seeking to carve out cultural space within a patriarchal denomination and in the face of the larger white supremacist culture.

This book is organized both chronologically and thematically, roughly following Kealing's invitation for matter "political, sociological, historical, archaeological, educational and philosophical." In keeping with Matthews's proclamations about the forms race literature would take, I arranged the selections based on three primary criteria: the historical understanding of these subjects at the time; the contributions in the *Review*'s "departments"; and thematic content. Most of the featured submissions were published up front in the quarterly, where major original features appeared. Only E. Marie Carter's long-running "Notes of Travel" appeared in the back pages (almost exclusively in the "Business" column).

Women indeed contributed to the "creation and transmission of literary culture," as Wills asserts, but they also appraised literature as well as other forms of culture, including art and music, which is the subject of chapter 1, "Beyond 'Creation and Transmission of Literary Culture.'" Although *transmission* implies a passive process of conveyance from one individual or group to another, these women contributors played an active role in analyzing and criticizing literary culture, thereby claiming cultural authority for AME churchwomen in particular and Black women more generally.

As Spires argues, during this era, the "practice of citizenship" implicitly had political overtones, and chapters 2–4 explore the politics evident in these writings.[28] Chapter 2, "AME Churchwomen Making History," discusses historical contributions, a category that includes the few pieces that were explicitly political in nature and those that mentioned political events or personages. Although until recently, "the study of racial thought [has] largely focused on men," African American women made contributions in this arena as well, not only presenting matter of historical importance but also signaling that in doing so, they were participating in American cultural history as purveyors of historical instruction.[29] Laurie F.

Maffly-Kipp and Kathryn Lofton as well as other scholars have identified race history as the predominant form of historical narrative contributed by Black women writers, and these women contributed biographies of historical figures, political histories, and analyses of historical eras that focused on Black women as well as men, including the authors' contemporaries.[30]

As Williams notes, the field of sociology was in its infancy and was often intertwined with social reform.[31] In this light, chapters 3 and 4 analyze "sociological" writings in the era's major areas of social reform. Chapter 3, "Sociological Writings: Home, Family, Church," and chapter 4, "Sociological Writings: Suffrage, Temperance, Crime, Prison Reform," treat both the women contributors who self-identified as ethnographers, sociologists, and social reformers and those whose work scholars of Black women's intellectual history now consider to have contributed to the emerging discourses of these disciplines during the Progressive Era. The elite white male gatekeepers of the field of sociology have historically resisted the construction of narrative histories of the discipline.[32] However, as Patricia Hill Collins, Delores P. Aldridge, and others have argued, Anna Julia Cooper, Frances Ellen Watkins Harper, Ida B. Wells-Barnett, and other nineteenth- and early twentieth-century Black women intellectuals engaged in both writing and activism that can be understood as sociological.[33] In addition, these women directly challenged their denomination's patriarchal theology by arguing for a wider sphere of influence not only for AME churchwomen but for all African American women.

Chapter 5, "E. Marie Carter's 'Notes of Travel' Column 1903–1912," fills a gap in what we know about Black travel writing between earlier book-length evangelistic travel narratives and the 1936 publication of Victor H. Green's *The Negro Motorist Green-Book*. Carter's faith-focused observations contrast with similar sociological writings by Du Bois, Wells-Barnett, and others, and by supplying the names and street addresses of homes and businesses she visited, Carter provided an "above-ground railroad" resource of sites that welcomed Black travelers during the Jim Crow era. Chapter 6, "Matters Educational," situates women's contributions to the *Review* within the history of Black education in the United States at all levels (Sunday schools, grammar schools, and elementary, secondary, and higher education). As Elizabeth McHenry, Gholdy Muhammad, Audrey Thomas McCluskey, Crystal Lynn Webster, Heather Andrea Williams, and others have demonstrated, even while enslaved, African Americans pursued educational opportunities for themselves and their children, and those efforts continued after emancipation through teaching others to read and write, building or providing space for schools, and starting literary societies.[34] At a time when few professions were open to Black women, teaching offered an opportunity for contributing to racial uplift through education. Some educated Black women proved eager not only to teach others but also to contribute to ongoing discourses about the role of race literature in racial uplift. Some women educators who contributed to the *Review* argued for both racially integrated and coeducational opportunities. Other contributors argued for either professional training for women (in law and medicine, for example) or training in the arts, including painting and music.

A few highly educated Black women contributed matter of a scientific or philosophical nature, and these contributions constitute the subject of chapter 7, "Matters Scientific and Philosophical." As Xine Yao reports, in 1890, just 15 of the 104,805 practicing physicians in the United States were African American women; a decade later, that number topped 100.[35] Two of these women physicians contributed articles on physiology and hygiene to the *Review*, and their submissions may have been motivated by "Enlightened Motherhood," an 1892 speech by Harper, a regular contributor to the *Review*. According to Yao, Harper established a model that empowered Black women "to bring literature and science together in the activism of everyday life."[36] Other women writers published articles focused on US geography or combined historical observations and philosophical speculation.

The volume concludes with a brief summary of how these women contributors responded to the historical and cultural challenges they faced and some thoughts about how future work on African American women's contributions to denominational periodicals might further our understanding of the development of race literature and Black intellectual history. Finally, the appendix lists the contributions from women authors during the period considered in this study.

CHAPTER 1

Beyond "Creation and Transmission of Literary Culture"

Women contributors did assist in the "creation and transmission" of literary culture, as David W. Wills has noted, by submitting poetry, fiction, and drama to the *A.M.E. Church Review*.[1] However, these authors also assumed active roles as critics, displaying their erudition in prose genres including linguistic histories, literary histories, literary biographies, literary criticism, translations, and book reviews as well as analyses of art and music. At a time when the AME Church's male preachers provided most of the spiritual instruction published in the *Review*, these prose essays created a cultural space in which women could share their thoughts on how exposure to these culture forms could help to develop Christian virtues. While none of these writings could be considered theological in the sense in which literary historian Joycelyn Moody uses the term, these essays demonstrate their authors' skill while simultaneously identifying qualities consistent with Christian piety.[2] The bulk of the essays focus on well-known white male writers of the Western literary canon, but rather than praising their literary accomplishments, the contributors recuperated the authors' lives in spiritual affinity with those of the women. Thus, their analyses focused on the men's life journeys rather than on their published work. A *Review* reader would not need to have read those writings to feel that affinity. Moreover, in discussions of Black authors, some contributors, among them Katherine Davis Tillman, resisted white male critics' assessments that reduced Black literature to stereotypes employing vernacular speech patterns.

Some of the lengthier contributions from women writers unabashedly lay out complex linguistic histories that seem to have served as shortened introductions to what readers might have encountered in college-level courses on the subject. Indeed, two of the earliest issues of the *Review* featured substantial prose contributions from college teachers. Josephine J. Turpin, a graduate of Howard University who later married Dr. Samuel Somerville Hawkins Washington and taught at Selma University, Tuskegee Institute, and Lincoln Normal School as well as at Howard, authored "The Origin and Progress of the English Language" (January 1885), while Sarah C. Bierce Scarborough, a faculty member at Wilberforce University, submitted the "The French Language of the Thirteenth Century" (July 1885).[3]

Turpin's five-page article traces the origins of the English language from Julius Caesar's invasion of England in 55 BC and the Roman encounter with the Celts through the arrival of the Anglo-Saxons and the influence of the Normans (French) to Chaucer, whom she pronounced "a great benefactor of the language" for giving to it "a definite form and permanence" (282). She credits the printing press and the Elizabethan age as "the greatest in the history of the English language," bemoans the "pernicious influence" of the restoration of Charles II, and credits the age of Pope with regularizing the "chaste and polished style" inherited by the Romantics and Victorians (283). Turpin concludes, "No language is so widely spoken as is English," asserting that "upon the future of the English-speaking people depends what the English language will be" (284). She seems to be citing this "chaste and polished style" as a model worthy of imitation by contributors to the *Review*, particularly women, who could thus display not only their erudition but also their piety.

According to Michele Valerie Ronnick, Sarah Cordelia Bierce was born in 1851 in Danby, New York, and trained at the Oswego Teaching Institute. After an early marriage to a former Union soldier and the birth of two sons (only one of whom survived), she fled the abusive marriage, earned her bachelor's degree in 1875, and headed south to teach for the American Missionary Society. While there she met Dr. William Sanders Scarborough, and the two joined the faculty of Wilberforce University in 1877 and married on July 31, 1881. He went on to become the school's president, while she served as principal of the Normal Department until 1914. Because William Scarborough was African American and Wilberforce is a historically Black university, many scholars have incorrectly assumed that Sarah Scarborough was Black. During her long career, she trained more than three hundred Black teachers who took jobs across the country and published nearly 150 works.[4]

Sarah Scarborough's eight-page history of the French language also begins with Julius Caesar's invasion of Gaul, which occurred at roughly the same time as the invasion of England. Scarborough focuses on the important shifts that occurred in the language during the thirteenth century, between the Old French period (fifth to twelfth centuries) and the Modern French period (which began in the 1400s). Drawing a parallel for her readers, she observes, "The French reader today needs as much assistance in reading that tale of love and chivalry—the Roman de la Rose . . . as the English reader requires to understand Chaucer's translation of the same" (47). In conclusion, Scarborough notes, "it must ever be a matter of regret, paradoxical as it may sound, that the fair form of the 13th century could not have been retained by the modern French" (51). Her detailed literary history served *Review* readers who perhaps had limited knowledge of the history of languages. Moreover, as a white woman, Scarborough's decades-long commitment to the educational endeavors of African Methodism at Wilberforce likely demonstrated the expanding denomination's widening embrace of a variety of races and ethnicities.[5]

Literary Histories

Turpin (who later published under her married name, Josephine J. Turpin Washington) contributed nearly a dozen prose pieces to the *A.M.E. Church Review* during this period, including "The Province of Poetry" (October 1889). As scholar Rita B. Dandridge notes, the teacher and journalist often quoted from the great authors of the Western literary tradition to argue for an upward trajectory in human progress that encompassed the uplift efforts of women and African Americans.[6] While many of Washington's essays directly address educational issues or the reform efforts of the blossoming women's club movement, the ten pages of "The Province of Poetry" lay out Washington's view of the form's place in literary history. Washington shares favorite passages from many classical British and American poets, insisting that poetry provides not only individual spiritual uplift that counteracts the soullessness of moneymaking, worldly pursuits but also a "humanitarian influence" that connects readers empathically to the needs of others as well as a "spiritualizing effect" that connects readers to the divine and the eternal.[7]

Washington begins the essay by noting that "all verse is not poetry" (137). After citing numerous writers about what poetry is, she provides her own definition: "Poetry is a species of composition, usually metrical in form, addressed especially to the imagination, and tending to please, instruct and inspire" (138). Noting that many "practical" men reject poetry as "sentimental," Washington distinguishes between a "sentimentality" that appeals to spurious tears and sentiment that encourages empathetic engagement with the suffering of others and "labors for its relief" (138). This concept of sentiment is consistent with what scholar Shirley Samuel identifies as America's "national project" and P. Gabrielle Foreman describes as the "political" thrust of much of "Black nineteenth-century sentimental . . . literary production."[8]

The middle portion of the essay relies on a series of aphorisms supported by exemplars from Washington's favorite poets: "Poets

FIGURE 1.1. MRS. JOSEPHINE TURPIN WASHINGTON. FROM THE NEW YORK PUBLIC LIBRARY DIGITAL COLLECTIONS.

are seers"; "Poetry has a particular charm for the lover of nature"; "Poetry is closely allied to our best affections"; "The whole aim of poetry . . . is to spiritualize the nature"; "Poetry takes us out of ourselves"; "Poetry is the divinest of all arts"; "All true poets are 'touched with a coal from heaven'"; "The poet is his own benefactor as well as ours"; "Does not humanity owe something to the poet? . . . But if mankind owes much to the poet, does not the poet owe much also to mankind?" (140–45). Although nearly all of the poets Washington quotes are men, she references two lines from Madame de Staël, includes a short unattributed passage from a Felicia Hemans poem, and concludes with thoughts inspired by an Elizabeth Barrett Browning piece that affirms Washington's final aphorism, "The poet is but the mouthpiece of 'God'" (147).[9] Washington thus links the poet to the divine as God's spokesperson, a view of the function of literature that likely resonated with *Review* readers.

Tillman also published several literary history essays in the *Review*. "The Negro Among Anglo-Saxon Poets" (July 1897), opens with a complaint that in the hands of contemporary white writers, African Americans appear as little more than faithful antebellum servants. But, Tillman argues, African Americans are becoming "soldiers, statesmen, poets, authors, financiers and reformers" (106), and any fiction focusing on Black characters ought to reflect those aspirations and achievements. Tillman finds precedent for more capacious rendering of Black characters in the work of Shakespeare (*Othello*) and of poets Browning ("The Runaway Slave at Pilgrim's Point"), John Greenleaf Whittier ("Toussaint L'Ouverture"), and Henry Wadsworth Longfellow ("The Warning"). Tillman closes by noting, "It is from perusing poems like these that our sorely tried spirits arise refreshed, and we are enabled to go on from 'strength to strength'" (112). Reading poems that center noble Black characters thus serves as a form of spiritual uplift, akin to listening to a sermon or reading a theological treatise by a clergyman.

In "Afro-American Poets and Their Verse" (April 1898), Tillman moves on from African Americans as poetic subjects to African Americans as poets. She opens with a quote from Wordsworth bemoaning the fact that many natural-born poets simply lack a youthful cultural environment in which to flourish, observing that this situation applies to members of the Black race. Tillman credits editor and literary critic William Dean Howells with bringing the reading public's attention to Paul Lawrence Dunbar's poetry. However, Tillman takes issue with Howells's contention that Dunbar's best work was in "humorous dialect verse," countering with *Review* editor Hightower T. Kealing's assessment that Dunbar's best work is yet to come (427). Acknowledging the cultural authority of the white male critic, Tillman nevertheless asserts that Dunbar—and by extension, all Black poets—are capable of much more than "humorous dialect verse."

Retracing ground likely familiar to regular *Review* readers, Tillman also cites Phyllis [sic] Wheatley, Frances Ellen Watkins Harper, Charlotte Grimké, Josephine Heard, H. Cordelia Ray, and Dunbar as accomplished Black poets. In addition, Tillman praises the poetry of such lesser-known authors as Alberry A. Whitman (whose "The Freedman's Triumphant Song" was read at the 1892 World's Fair), Robert Clayton (whose work appeared in *The Christian Recorder*), Dr. H. T. Johnson (editor of *The Christian Recorder*), and a half dozen others whose work appeared in the *Review*. Tillman ends by thanking the editors of Black journals for publishing these works and opining that "with riper scholarship," Black poets will make significant contributions to world literature (428).

Like the contributions of Washington and Tillman, journalist and activist Gertrude Bustill Mossell's "Life and Literature" (January 1898) allows her to infuse an essay on literature with religious musings. Mossell cites definitions of her subject matter—in this case, life—offered by other authors before arriving at her own statement on the topic. She asserts that each life is individual, a gift from "The Divine," and that "each soul" has "its own mission to perform" (318–19). These words likely resonated with readers familiar with the language of the AME Church's foundational text, *The Doctrine and Discipline of the African Methodist Episcopal Church*. Mossell goes on to distinguish among the "life physical," the "life moral," the "life intellectual," and the "life spiritual," all of which require daily nurturance for the soul to reach its full potential—"man's true or ideal life" (319). Since life is a mission, she argues, each individual must choose a worthy line of work and "pursue it unceasingly" in the company of loved ones (319). Noting that in former ages, man lived for "himself," then for his "kinsfolk," then for his "race," and finally for his "nation" (320), Mossell argues that men have now come to recognize the potential in all human lives (322), a shift she credits to "Literature"—principally to the "one book" that presents "the Word of God" but also all books that "move the hearts of men" (322).

Asserting that humanity can come to know and love "only those nations whose literature we have studied," Mossell urges readers not to "undervalue the worth" of "race literature" (325). However, Mossell's description of race literature looks back rather than toward the future Matthews envisions. Mossell specifically mentions the

Figure 1.2. Mrs. Josephine Silone Yates. From the New York Public Library Digital Collections.

songs sung by aging nurses to their charges, the songs of the enslaved in the field, and the folklore handed down, which she describes as the outpourings of a race literature still in its infancy (325). She urges "spokesmen" to rise to the occasion of creating literary works worthy of the race's "true biography, its true history" (325). Whereas Mossell's "The Colored Woman in Verse" (July 1885; see chapter 2) catalogs past Black achievements, her 1898 essay invokes a more philosophical call to current and future Black authors to produce literature worthy of consideration alongside other great world literatures.

Josephine Silone Yates contributed a four-part series on French Literature that concluded in the January 1901 issue of the *Review*.[10] Complementing Scarborough's earlier article on French linguistic history, Yates contributed more than forty pages of prose to the journal, an amount surpassed only by E. Marie Carter, whose long-running travel column totaled 160 pages between 1903 and 1912 (see chapter 5). The decision to feature these linguistic and literary histories suggests that the editors of the *A.M.E. Church Review* sought to showcase the educational accomplishments of women contributors, a practice that reached its zenith with the January 1901 issue in which all the contributors were women.

LITERARY BIOGRAPHY

Literary scholar Daniel Hack persuasively argues that "nineteenth-century British literature was woven deeply into the fabric of nineteenth- and early twentieth-century African American literature and print culture."[11] This idea is evident in the literary biographies and literary criticism contributed by women writers to the *Review* prior to and during the first years of Kealing's editorship, likely because Kealing was an educator rather than a clergyman and consequently encouraged longer literary/historical contributions. While their male counterparts submitted literary biographies and criticism on Homer, Bunyan, Shakespeare, Condorcet, Whittier, Poe, and Tolstoy, women authors contributed biographies of Dickens, Lamb, Thoreau, Pope, Longfellow, Dumas, and Pushkin as well as literary criticism on Longfellow's "Evangeline," Schiller's "Die Beiden Piccolomini," Milton's "Paradise Lost," and Tacitus's *Germania*.[12] Women contributors not only assessed the stylistic attributes of authors and literature but usually also commented on the authors' moral and spiritual qualities, consistent with aligning these qualities with the contributors' practices of piety.

A prime example of this strategy is Turpin's seven-page biography, "Charles Dickens" (July 1885). Turpin opens by noting that Dickens's father retired from naval service to become a reporter and that Charles received scant childhood education before becoming a reporter for the House of Commons (34, 35). Turpin credits Dickens's success as a writer to his "voracious" reading habit as a young man. Turpin mentions most of Dickens's major works but devotes particular attention to "American Notes for General Circulation," which Dickens released after an 1842 tour of the United States during which he attacked the institution of slavery, and observes that he reiterated this fierce criticism in his next novel, *Martin Chuzzlewit* (36). Also important is her analysis of Dickens's character: "While he never openly professed Christianity . . . he had a profound reverence for all things sacred. His was the creed of a noble life" (40).

As in the later "Lessons from the Life of McKinley" (January 1902), Turpin uses this essay to praise personal traits worth of emulation, describing Dickens as "industrious" and "methodical in his habits" and alluding to the temperance cause by adding that he never used "a stimulant of any kind" during his working hours. Finally, Turpin notes that Dickens's works "effected important reforms" in eliciting "sympathy for the lowly," making his life a suitable model for "literature-loving people," especially the *Review*'s African American readers (40).

H. Cordelia Ray, noted by her peers for her carefully crafted poetry, contributed "Charles Lamb" (July 1891), which served as the issue's lead article. Ray focuses on Lamb's ability to overcome adversity and on his close relationship with his sister, Mary, for whom he served as a caregiver. Ray may well have been drawn to Lamb's life story because it resembled her own. Well known in African American literary circles of the day, Henrietta Cordelia Ray was the daughter of Charles Bennett Ray, a Congregational minister and an editor of *The Colored American*, an abolitionist newspaper. Cordelia and her sisters were well educated: Cordelia graduated from the University of the City of New York in 1891 and was fluent in several languages, while her younger sister Charlotte graduated from Howard University Law School and was admitted to the bar. Cordelia and another sister, Florence, taught public school for a time, but Cordelia found that teaching did not suit her, so she spent the majority of her mature years reading, writing, and caring for her sister.[13]

Ray observes that both Charles and Mary Lamb suffered from bouts of mental illness requiring institutionalization but that Charles nevertheless forged deep friendships with many of the esteemed authors of his day: Coleridge, Shelley, Keats, Hunt, Wordsworth, and others (6). In analyzing Lamb's "genius," Ray points to his "keen insight" as a humorist and his "rare discrimination" as a critic (8). She praises his sentences as "pithy, epigrammatic, impressive" and notes that Coleridge pronounced Lamb's reputation the least likely to diminish (8). While Ray discusses many of Lamb's best-known works (including the essays he wrote under the pen name Elia), she focuses the latter portion of her essay on an examination of "a more sacred sphere"—Lamb's "inner nature" (8). Despite his "pathetic loneliness" and his "mercurial temperament," Lamb was "always unconsciously drawn toward those in adversity" (8) and displayed complete "brotherly devotion" to Mary (9). As a result, Ray concludes, Lamb led a "saintly" life and future generations would remember him not merely as "a genial humorist and critic, but as a noble soul" (9).

Sarah Elizabeth Miller Tanner, the wife of Benjamin T. Tanner, editor of *The Christian Recorder* and the *A.M.E. Church Review*, contributed two literary biographies to the quarterly during this period: "A Study of Thoreau" (January 1895) and "Henry Wadsworth Longfellow" (October 1895).[14] Much about Thoreau's life renders him an unlikely candidate for Tanner's attention: she notes that he never married, never went to church, and never voted. However, she also notes that he "drank no wine," eschewed tobacco, and never used a gun (383).

Tanner describes Thoreau as a "political iconoclast" (383), a phenomenon she credits to his varied ancestry: his "Puritan blood" gave him a strong "sense of justice"; his Scots blood led to his embrace of "unsubdued manliness"; his Jersey forebears made him resistant to tax collection; and his French heritage bestowed on him a preference for "revolution at any time" over biding the outcomes of the present (384). Thoreau's commitment to "individual rights" (384) and his opposition to slavery (386) render him as an "Idealist," according to his friend Emerson, but also mark his character as worth studying. Like Turpin

Figure 1.3. Mrs. Sarah E. Tanner. From the New York Public Library Digital Collections.

and Ray, Tanner uses the genre of literary biography to advocate for temperance and to highlight qualities she finds desirable in all men, regardless of race. Her description of the benefits of his varied ethnic heritage also undercuts white fears of racial and ethnic mixing.

Tanner's eight-page biographical essay on Longfellow emphasizes the professional attainments available to those who pursue advanced education. The essay opens with several quotations and observations from his contemporaries on Longfellow's character: "gentle, docile, cheerful, intelligent" (Charles Elliott Norton), "self-disciplining" (Rev. George Y. Packard), and "much honored in the community" of Portland, Maine, where he grew up (his brother Samuel) (283). By taking advantage of educational opportunities, Longfellow landed a professorship at Bowdoin College (285) and subsequently the chair of modern languages at Harvard (287). Education proved particularly important in the Tanner household: Sarah and Benjamin's eldest daughter, Hallie Tanner Johnson, became a physician, while one of their sons, Carl, was a minister and another, Henry, was a renowned artist.[15]

The January 1895 issue of the *Review* also contained another biography, "Alexander Pope," written by Selena C. Lake.[16] Lake's piece proves as acerbic as Pope's reputed wit, a characteristic that she attributes in part to his "crooked form," an inheritance from his father (388). She notes that his "Pastorals" demonstrate "but little originality" and "can hardly be regarded otherwise than a schoolboy's exercises" (389): "to the reader of this day his poignancy and vituperations are but little enjoyed" (389). She bemoans the low opinion of women evident in "Rape of the Lock," noting that the poet suffered "the common masculine weakness of self approbation" (390, 392). Lake thus offered subtle critiques of both white male presumed superiority and her denomination's paternalistic and patriarchal attitude toward women. More positively, she observes that Pope "climbed the ladder of success" through his "high ambition" and attributes his vitriolic nature to a paucity of female companionship, which might have served to "soften his disposition" (393). Such comments about the elevating effect of female companionship suggest that she had nascent feminist leanings. Lake concludes by noting that at Pope was surrounded by faithful friends as he left behind his "misshapen mortal tabernacle" to ascend to immortality. She muses that perhaps on his deathbed, Pope meditated on the words of his poem "The Dying Christian to His Soul": "Cease fond nature, cease thy strife / And let me languish into life" (394). Lake thus positions Pope's biography within a narrative of Christian spiritual redemption.

Two additional literary biographies penned by Tillman, "Alexandre Dumas, Pére" (January 1907) and "Alexander Sergeivich Pushkin" (July 1909) recuperate these well-known authors within a larger race history honoring writers of African descent. Tillman boldly takes aim at white writers who despair of the calamity of "amalgamation" by pointing out that Dumas, "greatest French romantic novelist," was the grandson of an African American woman from Hispaniola (257). Moreover, when given the option of taking the name of his illustrious grandfather, a nobleman from the house of Davy de la Piolleterie, Alexandre chose his father's name, Dumas (238). After arriving in Paris, Dumas became acquainted with Victor Hugo and other well-known French writers, eventually following Hugo to Brussels after Louis Napoleon's ascension to the throne in 1851. Tillman closes with words borrowed from earlier biographers: Dumas was "both a black man and a white man; a Royalist and a Republican; an aristocrat and a Sans-Culotte" who belonged not only to France or to Europe but to the world (262–63). Echoing Tanner, Tillman seeks to defuse fears of racial mixing by recasting Dumas's dual nature as one basis for his literary gifts to the larger world.

Tillman's biography of Pushkin opens similarly, noting that "the poet, regardless of his nationality, becomes the common property of mankind" (27). She places Pushkin alongside Homer, Virgil, Khayyam, Goethe, Hugo, Burns, Chaucer, Shakespeare, Poe, Longfellow, Dunbar, and others, querying, "Who, while listening to the melody and rhythm of Dunbar's verse cares that he was a Negro?" (27). She chooses to write about Pushkin because he is little-known in America and because he "is of Negro descent and in our country would be classed a Negro" (28). Again echoing Tanner, Tillman admits to a "deep interest in the study of heredity," prefacing her remarks on Pushkin with a detailed analysis of an unnamed close friend with roots in Africa, Germany, and Kentucky (28). Pushkin was a descendant of Ibrahim Hannibal, an African sent to Peter the Great as a gift (29). Although pronounced "very stupid" as a child, Pushkin learned from tutors hired by his father and later attended college at the Tsarky [sic] Selo Lyceum (29). Although Pushkin was well received in Moscow literary circles, he wrote his best work—a series of national poems—only after returning to Tsarky [sic] Selo (31).

After noting that Pushkin's political positions made him many enemies and that he was killed in an 1837 duel, Tillman closes by quoting Pushkin's "An Eastern Song": "Ah, thou wert born for languid pleasures / And glowing hours of bliss divine" (32). As in her essay on Dumas, Tillman here offers a gentle rebuttal to those who harbored deep-seated fears about the dangers of racial mixing, stressing that racial mixing is already common in other nations and has produced men of great talent. The *Review*'s long-standing practice of exchanging material with leading white-run publications meant that the journal's contributors wrote for white as well as Black readers.

Literary Criticism and Book Reviews

As was the case throughout the *Review* during this period, men authored most of the journal's literary criticism and book reviews. The first editor, Benjamin T. Tanner initiated two columns, "Our Book Table" and "Our Reviews," that appeared regularly at the end of most issues of the quarterly. Under the editorship of Levi Coppin, these columns became "Book Reviews and Comments" and "Magazines and Reviews" and were handled either by the editor himself or by an assistant. Kealing continued these columns with some slight modifications in titles and content and added a new column, "Miscellaneous," that sometimes contained original material but often featured excerpts from other publications, including literature reviews. All three of these editors positioned longer works of literary criticism and book reviews submitted by women contributors near the front of the quarterly. The fourth editor, Reverdy C. Ransom, was more concerned with supplying matter suitable for the education and training of the denomination's ministerial corps and consequently created a new section devoted to literary criticism, "Within the Sphere of Letters," at the end of the quarterly, and it became the sole province of George W. Forbes, an employee of the Boston Public Library. Ransom continued to publish serial and short fiction authored by women, but most of these contributors' longer works of literary criticism, book reviews, literary translations, and art and music reviews appeared prior to his tenure.

Frazelia Campbell authored three essays of literary criticism ("Die Beiden Piccolomini" [January 1885]; "Tacitus' German Women" [July 1885]; and "Milton's Satan" [October 1890]) as well as a philosophical essay. Lillian Viola Thompson also published an essay of literary criticism, "Beauties in Evangeline" (July 1890).

Campbell was born on March 18, 1849, in Charleston, South Carolina, graduated from Philadelphia's Institute for Colored Youth in Philadelphia in 1867, and immediately began teaching Latin, German, and Spanish there. In 1876, she became principal of institute's girls high school, a position she held until 1902, when the school became a normal and industrial school. In 1880, she was living with her mother, Julia Campbell, and three siblings on South Street in Philadelphia. After teaching for some time at Allen University in Columbia, South Carolina, Campbell returned to Philadelphia, where she died on October 5, 1930.[17]

In "Die Beiden Piccolomini," Campbell assesses the second section of Friedrich Schiller's three-part drama, *Wallenstein*. She chose Schiller because both his character and his poetry displayed "noble principles," a "lofty imagination," and "Christian virtues" (200). A historical drama, "Die Beiden Piccolomini" is set during the Thirty Years' War (1618–48), when the titular character, Max Piccolomini, is caught among the shifting powers in General Wallenstein's camp. Campbell finds Max's speeches the most compelling portion of the drama because they best embody Schiller's "ideas of national freedom and peace-loving sentiments" (203). In the fictionalized relationship between Max and his love, Thekla, Campbell sees Schiller's "idea of human perfection" realized, and she pronounces Max a character that Shakespeare "could not possibly have formed" (203). The few scenes with Max and Thekla constitute the "chief beauties" of the drama and "much that attracts the general reader" (204).

In "Tacitus' German Women," Campbell specifically refutes an article by Elizabeth Cady Stanton, "Has Christianity Benefitted Women?" published in the *North American Review* in 1885. Campbell's disagreement with Stanton may have been rooted in her shifting position regarding suffrage for African American women, but Campbell notes other reviewers who took issue with some of Stanton's claims and specifically counters the assertion that the improved treatment of women can be traced to Germanic influences rather than to Christianity. Citing the historian Tacitus's work *Germania*, Campbell asserts that German women had always been treated as "household drudges" (168) and that "the German obtained his wife as he would any other marketable commodity. He bought her" (169)—that is, he paid rather than received a dowry. Campbell bolsters her argument by referring to several other authorities on German culture and by pointing out that "the institutions of learning in Germany" still "close their doors to the women" (172). Campbell concludes with a suggestion that the earnestness of German women coupled with the broad philanthropy of American women might initiate further reform in both countries (173).

In "Milton's Satan," Campbell takes the poet to task for creating a character so "thrilling and magnificent" that young, untutored readers might want to emulate him (196). Like many of her sister contributors to the *Review*, Campbell places piety over artistic genius. Because Milton presents the "enemy of mankind" as a hero, even "readers of well-balanced moral discernment" might find themselves subject to "strong fascinations" (196). Both Milton's Satan and Aeschylus's Prometheus display an "unfearing, unconquerable will" (196), a depiction Campbell attributes to Milton's rebelliousness, lofty enthusiasm, and strong individuality, characteristics that might lead young readers to adopt bad behaviors that might be hard to later correct (198). She suggests reading the work of Dickens, whose "shocking" villains such as Uriah Heep will "arouse a hatred for depravity" (198).

"Beauties in Evangeline" exemplifies the *Review*'s occasional practice of showcasing the work of student writers from Wilberforce University and other educational institutions. Thompson graduated from New York's Public School No. 67 in 1889, and her essay is based on the valedictory address she delivered at the school's

June 28 commencement.[18] "Beauties in Evangeline" is more of a plot summary and lacks the polish of the other literary criticism published in the journal. According to Thompson, "Nearly everyone with sensibilities above those of an invertebrate has, at some period of his existence, experienced rich spiritual enjoyment, divine sympathies, sacred thrills," and many who fall under Cupid's spell find themselves engaged in "the stubborn fight of baffled desire" (54). Such is the situation in which Evangeline Bellefontaine and her love, Gabriel Lajeunesse, find themselves. The essay's focus on "baffled desire" suggests the concerns of a young woman coming to maturity within a religious denomination with strict matrimonial requirements.[19] *Review* editors likely published the work of student writers to encourage the race's next generation of would-be scholars and leaders as well as to remind them of the need for chastity and piety, particularly among young women.

During this period, women contributed only two reviews of recently released books or pamphlets: a review of George Washington Cable's *Dr. Sevier* (October 1888) by "Miss H. A. Rice" and Mary Louisa Mossell's review of Henry Drummond's *The Greatest Thing in the World* (April 1892).

Rice's review opens with a critique of four contemporary writers, including Henry James, whose work she dismisses as "long drawn-out society novels, tales of foolish women and insipid men," and Joel Chandler Harris, whose pages of "utterly inane and wearisome dialect" she cannot abide (149). Rice finds *Dr. Sevier* not as fully realized as Cable's collection of short stories *Old Creole Days* but nonetheless praises his "lightness and naturalness of style" (149). Rice declares Mary, a young woman whom Dr. Sevier tries to assist, "the best thing in the book," displaying "patience and faith and hope" in the face of the failures of her ambitious but misguided husband (151). However, Rice concedes, the book "is not well-constructed," the tale lacks "unity," and the character of the beautiful young man Narcisse is completely unnecessary (152). In an unusual criticism for an article in a religious quarterly, Rice chides the author for being "an earnest Christian": the "expression of religious faith is all very well in Sunday school books" but is "out of place" in a novel.

More in keeping with the other literary articles in the *Review* is Mossell's piece on the Drummond's thirty-two-page pamphlet. Mary Louisa Tanner, the daughter of *Review* editor Tanner and his wife, Sarah Elizabeth Miller Tanner, married Aaron Albert Mossell, the first Black graduate of the University of Pennsylvania, in 1890. Aaron Mossell subsequently earned a law degree and was admitted to the bar in 1895. Originally from Ontario, Canada, he was the brother of Nathan Francis Mossell, a physician who was married to Gertrude Bustill Mossell, author of *The Work of the Afro-American Woman* and a contributor to the *Review*.[20]

The review of *The Greatest Thing in the World* opens with Mary Louisa Mossell's assessment (with which such other publications as *The Independent* and *The Religious Telescope* concurred) that the work has "especial merit" and that she feels it her duty to tell others about it. Drummond begins with the text from St. Paul's first letter to the Corinthians in which he asserts that of "faith, hope, charity . . . the greatest of these is charity" (400). Some translations substitute *love* for *charity*, so Mossell takes love to be the "greatest thing" of the pamphlet's title and moves section by section through Drummond's argument praising its superiority. Mossell also notes that "the prayerful, earnest Christian seeks at once to fit" all of these qualities "into his character" and observes that reading the pamphlet regularly and prayerfully may change "one's whole life." Although the AME Church's *Doctrine and Discipline* specified that male members and clergy should read almost exclusively Scripture and scriptural exegesis, the denomination's guidelines for its women's auxiliary organizations encouraged meetings to allow women "time to read original poems" and "lectures upon the various subjects connected to life," a category that would have included *The Greatest Thing in the World*.[21]

Translations

Two women writers contributed English translations of foreign literature during this period: Scarborough submitted a translation of French poet Alphonse de Lamartine's tribute to Haitian rebel Toussaint-Louverture (October 1887). And Gertrude Amelia Mahorney contributed "Christmas Eve" (October 1899), a translation of a German tale by Johann Ludwig Tieck. According to historian Steven R. Barnett, Mahorney was the first Black student to earn bachelor's and master's degrees from Indiana's Butler University, and she went on to teach in the state's Black schools in the early 1900s.[22]

Scarborough chose a portion of Lamartine's poem in which Toussaint-Louverture rallies his troops while they hide atop a mountain awaiting Napoleon's soldiers: "The moment's come with us to sting in heel / Th' oppressor race now crushing us—Come then!" (158). The two and half pages of Scarborough's translation include Toussaint-Louverture's memory of a gruesome scene in which a tiger dug up the graves of enslaver and enslaved and consumed the corpses, leaving only their skeletons. Toussaint-Louverture notes that the white body can no longer be distinguished from the Black: "Same bones, same senses, equal all—alike! / Said I ... Where, then, the diff'rence 'twixt the two?" (160). Scarborough thus highlights the absurdity of racial difference based on skin color and asserts the equality of the races in the eyes of God.

"Christmas Eve" is a moral tale about a family torn apart by greed and ambition. The narrator, a poor seamstress living with her young daughter in Berlin, explains that her husband's fiery temperament drove away their eldest son. Wanting his son to be a scholar, the father gave him expensive books (229–32). However, the son wished to be a merchant, a bloody confrontation ensued, and the son went to sea, where it was reported that he eventually perished (234). The father also died, and his reckless spending left his wife and young daughter paupers (235). The mother has saved one dollar to buy her daughter a Christmas present, but when they go out to spend the money on Christmas Eve, they cannot find it and must return home empty-handed (236). A man with a deeply scarred face has been shadowing them, but he knocks at their door and reveals that he is the long-lost son, who has become a wealthy merchant (238). Throughout the tale, the daughter has counseled her mother to remain faithful to the Christ child, and the piece concludes with the girl saying, "I was right. Our Savior, the invisible one, does sometimes come himself to our poor little homes" (240). The tale, an inversion of the Prodigal Son parable from the Gospel of Luke, would have provided suitable reading for readers' family circles during the holiday season, highlighting the importance of education, the dangers of greed and anger, and the need to maintain Christian faith in the face of life's trials and tribulations.

Artistic Cultures

Finally, women submitted two pieces analyzing artistic culture—specifically, music and art. Lucinda B. Bragg contributed "Music, and Woman's Relation to It," (April 1887), while Mrs. A. N. Johnston penned "The Greatest Pictures of the World" (April 1910). Bragg was a resident of Petersburg, Virginia, and had studied at the city's Virginia Normal and Industrial Institute, founded in 1882. As a student, she had composed music for "Old Blandford Church" and dedicated it to John Mercer Langston, who served as the institute's first president in 1886–87 and who in 1888 became the first African American elected to Congress from Virginia. Bragg became a teacher at St. Michael's Training and Industrial School for the Colored Race at Charlotte, North Carolina, and subsequently served as an assistant editor of *The Musical Messenger*, the earliest Black periodical dedicated solely to music.[23]

In "Music, and Woman's Relation to It," Bragg admits that her article provides "nothing new or original" but explains that she simply seeks "to collect such facts, combined with our views, to show music's power and woman's relation to it" (381). Her five-page article begins by tracing the history of music as an art form to ancient Greece and goes on to note that St. Ambrose systemized sacred chants in the church in the fourth century and that St. Gregory invented the eight-note scale in the seventh century (377). The invention of moveable type during the Reformation greatly enhanced the publication and distribution of music and made possible the careers of the great (male) composers of Europe, for whom women served primarily as inspiration and support (378–80). The article's final section, "Woman as an Interpreter of Music," turns to the women singers and musicians who rose to popularity beginning in the eighteenth century, with Bragg contending that they needed three qualities to achieve success: a grand voice, musical intelligence, and a pleasing appearance (381). Bragg concludes, "Man may be the intellect of music, but woman is its heart and soul" (381).

"The Greatest Pictures of the World" is likely the work of Lillian J. Johnson of Nashville, Tennessee, whose husband, Andrew N. Johnson, ran a successful mortuary business there.[24] The *Review* had relocated from Philadelphia to Nashville in January 1909 for "financial reasons" (January 1909, 343), and Kealing likely became acquainted with the Johnsons soon thereafter. The city's leading Black newspaper, *The Nashville Globe*, reported that Lillian Johnson served as vice president of the Fleur De Lis Art and Study Club, and this article may have begun as a paper she presented there.[25] Alternatively, the interest in art that resulted in the writing of this article may have prompted Johnson to form the club. The nine-page article, a compilation of the views of "acknowledged critics" (328) in the art world rather than of Johnson's personal experience, catalogs nearly eighty works by well-known French, Italian, Flemish, Spanish, German, English, and American artists, providing more extended discussion of her particular favorites and concluding with Longfellow's observation that "the artist never dies." Johnson's contribution demonstrates the ways in which African American women's club work and their religious lives were often inseparable.

The women contributors to the *A.M.E. Church Review* thus did not restrict themselves solely to the "creation and transmission of literary culture"; instead, they carved out cultural space for themselves as artistic and literary critics, historians, sociologists, travel writers, educators, and philosophers. They praised what they found spiritually uplifting, thereby not only demonstrating their own piety but encouraging pious pursuits on the part of their readers. In addition, some authors used their submissions to challenge racial and gender stereotypes.

CHAPTER 2

AME Churchwomen Making History

Like many of their male contemporaries, women contributors to the *A.M.E. Church Review* during this period created and submitted historical writings for publication in multiple genres, including poetry and drama, but this chapter focuses on prose essays. These authors used these works not only to write themselves into established narratives of Black history but also to demonstrate their ability to assume the mantle of historian, which at the time was generally reserved for men. They were thus making history in both senses of the expression. In the words of scholars Laurie F. Maffly-Kipp and Kathryn Lofton, "Whether in schoolrooms or kitchens, state houses or church pulpits, women have always been historians" despite their lack of access to the "academic study of history."[1]

As Maffly-Kipp and Lofton document, African American women's historical writings during the century prior to the Harlem Renaissance constitute "renderings of a racial past."[2] In addition, however, women writers produced and circulated other forms of historical writing: biographies of white as well as Black citizens, catalogs of contemporary race leaders (particularly women), and reportage of contemporary events.

These historical writings concerned topics directly related to the AME Church, such as its role in mission work in places such as Haiti, Bermuda, and South Africa, as well as broader subjects, including notables Abraham Lincoln, William McKinley, Crispus Attucks, and the Russian czars. Historical writings also addressed specific eras, such as "The Sixteenth Century in the Education of Modern Thought" (July 1903) and "Political Results of the Reformation" (April 1896) as well as the contributions of African American men and women to the shaping of American and diasporic histories. Taken together, these historical writings demonstrate an intellectual cosmopolitanism interested in literary, political, and militaristic development across the globe. And in many cases, women contributors used their writings to compare the oppressed in other countries and the plight of Black citizens in the United States.[3]

Quasi-Political Histories

Mrs. H. R. Noble contributed one of the few explicitly political essays, "Fetes for the Czar in Paris" (January 1897), which reads like a news report. Noble describes an October 1896 Parisian visit by Czar Nicholas II and Empress Alexandra, a granddaughter of Queen Victoria. Positioning herself among the gentry, Noble complains about the "class of people now in the city" who "gape and stare and pause and stare again, making street movements extremely difficult" (312). Noble attended a "balcony party" and watched a grand parade "down the beautiful Champs Elysees" that included not only the czar but also "African-Chasseurs and Arab shecks [sic] from Algiers . . . riding pure-blooded Arabian horses." It was, Noble declares, "the loveliest sight which I have seen during my two years travel in Europe" (313–14). By observing and writing about this event, which likely reflected the continuing public fascination with Victoria and her progeny, Noble establishes elite Black women as observers and chroniclers of history in the making.

An article by Victoria Earle, "The Crispus Attucks Monument" (April 1889), represents a hybrid contribution, both a look back at the start of the American Revolution and reportage of a contemporary event—the November 14, 1888, unveiling of the monument in Boston. Earle begins with an account of the March 5, 1770, Boston Massacre, when British soldiers fired into a crowd, killing several people, including the enslaved, mixed-race Attucks, who was memorialized as the first casualty of the revolution. Earle uses her retelling of historical events as well as her description of the statue and the festivities surrounding its unveiling to argue for the centrality of an African American to the nation's founding. Beneath Attucks's name, the monument bears the names of four white men killed in the incident, and Earle opines that they "mingled their blood with his, not as four white men and one colored, but as five unarmed patriots brutally charged upon by insolent, cowardly British soldiers" (388).[4] Earle thus argues for the victims' common humanity and elides racial differentiation.

Josephine Silone Yates was a frequent contributor of lengthy and deeply researched essays published under her own name as well as under her nom de plume, R. K. Potter. She studied at the Institute for Colored Youth in Philadelphia, directed by Fanny Jackson Coppin, and at Rhode Island State Normal School, where she graduated with honors in 1879. From 1881 to 1889, she taught at the Lincoln Institute in Jefferson City, Missouri, before leaving to marry William W. Yates, principal of the Wendell Phillips School in Kansas City. She contributed to the leading Black periodicals of the day, including *The Southern Workman, The Voice of the Negro, The Woman's Era, The Indianapolis Freeman*, and *The Kansas City Rising Sun*. Yates was also active in the founding of the National Association of Colored Women and was elected the organization's president in 1901.[5]

While Yates's subject matter ranged widely and included French literature and physical geography, political history (couched in the guise of religious history) proved especially fertile ground for her pen. In "Political Results of the Reformation" (April 1896), she argues for an "evolutionary" view of the concept of "liberty" in human history. She complains that most histories of the Reformation unfold as if Martin Luther "alone presided at its great first birth" (474). But, she argues, "there could have been no reformation in the accepted sense of the term if the minds of men had not been previously, fully awakened to a sense of dissatisfaction with their environments" (474). In Yates's interpretation of events, the German people, dissatisfied with the lack of reform under Emperor Maximilian I, sought a change in the authorized religion after centuries of being "crushed by the Church and impoverished by the nobility" (478). Luther was important to this movement but was only propelled along by the vast masses seeking change.

Yates then traces the spread of this Protestant movement beyond Germany to other parts of Europe and ultimately "across the sea to America" (479). In seeking "a new country," these Protestants hoped to "build up institutions grounded from the start upon the principles of liberty" (479). Touting "Liberty" as the "triumphant song of the Nineteenth Century" (481), she nonetheless notes that in the United States, the Reformation remains incomplete: "We still think somewhat disparagingly of any form of religion differing from our own, while the recent attempt in certain sections of our own country to disfranchise a portion of the legally voting population indicate that man has not yet attained the highest conception of a Reformation" (480). Yates thereby uses religious history to attack the southern states for disenfranchising Black voters.

Biographical Histories

Both biographies of individuals and group "race biographies" also proved popular in the *Review*. Josephine J. Turpin Washington's "Lessons from the Life of McKinley" (January 1902), published less than six months after the president's assassination, extols his virtues in terms designed to provide a role model for African American male readers. Washington, a graduate of the Richmond Theological Seminary and Howard University, worked as a teacher before her marriage to Dr. Samuel H. Washington. She began contributing to newspapers and magazines in 1877 and published nearly a dozen pieces—poetry, essays, and texts of speeches—to the *Review*.[6]

"Lessons from the Life of McKinley" praises the president's "diligent application," noting that he was "a self-made man" (211). She cites his "noble sincerity" and his "conscientious motives" but wishes that he had offered "a direct and vigorous denunciation of the horrors being perpetrated upon the Negro in the South" (211–12). Washington further praises McKinley's devotion to his "invalid wife" and "aged mother" as well as his "Christian living, . . . faith in God and submission to his will": "Through all historic time the impress of his life will be for good upon the lives of succeeding generations of Americans—and not upon Americans alone" (214). Washington cleverly eulogizes a historic white leader in terms that describe the ideal characteristics for which Black men should strive, a species of prescriptive literature that appeared far less frequently in the *Review* pages than did articles describing the traits of virtuous African American wives and mothers.

In another biographical essay, "Lincoln, the Emancipator" (April 1910), Yates adopts the rhetorical stance of a historian, foregrounding the intellectual labor involved in crafting historical narratives: "Historical records present to us an unbroken line of illustrious heroes, lofty in thought, dignified in speech, marvelous in action" (335). Yates both consults historical records and uses them to craft a new historical narrative. The *Review* published nearly a dozen articles on Abraham Lincoln between 1884 and 1923, but Yates's piece is the only one whose author was a woman. She declares that Lincoln is to the United States as Pericles was to Greece, Caesar to Rome, and Napoleon to France before devoting the rest of her ten-page treatise to Lincoln's step-by-step advancement of emancipation efforts between 1861 and 1863, "a chapter more thrilling and exciting than the pages of the most highly wrought fiction" (335). Yates quotes liberally from Lincoln's letters and public proclamations, leading her readers through the unfolding events that culminated in the Emancipation Proclamation and ultimately in the abolition of slavery. She closes by noting that while "American citizens" celebrate July 4 as Independence Day, "American Negroes" celebrate their "deliverance from political bondage" on Lincoln's "natal day" (344).

Race Histories

As Maffly-Kipp and Lofton note, most early American "race histories" depicted the accomplishments of African American men, but the 1890s saw the development of race histories by and about women such as Susan Elizabeth Frazier and Gertrude Bustill Mossell.[7] Among the women who contributed such race histories to the *Review* were Katherine Davis Tillman, Fannie C. Bentley, Julie K. Wetherill, and Ida Upshaw. In *Beyond Respectability*, Brittney C. Cooper labels this practice *listing*: "African American women created lists of prominent, qualified Black women for public consumption." According to Cooper, this practice constitutes more than "mere racial self-congratulations"; rather, "race women used listing not only as a practice to combat their historical exclusion but also to resist sexism, theorize about racial politics, and even gesture toward the kinds of political priorities that mattered based on the fields of work of the Black women they highlighted."[8] Listing certainly proved popular in the pages of the *Review*. In "The Woman's Christian Temperance Union and the Colored Woman" (January 1888) and "National Woman's Christian Temperance Union" (January 1889), Frances Ellen Watkins Harper used reportage regarding the anti-liquor movement to list by name and geographical location other Black women prominent in reform, thus writing her sisters into African American race history.

Mossell's earliest biographical work published in the *Review*, "The Colored Woman in Verse" (July 1885), represents an early version of "The Afro-American Woman in Verse," an essay included in her 1894 collection, *The Work of the Afro-American Woman*.[9] Frazier's "Some Afro-American Women of Mark" (April 1892) was the quarterly's second feature article, followed by such articles as "Woman's Exalted Station" and "Our Civil Rights." In addition, Tillman contributed "Afro-American Women and Their Work" (April 1895), "The Negro Among Anglo-Saxon Poets" (July 1897), and "Afro-American Poets and Their Verse" (April 1898), essays included in the Schomburg edition of *The Works of Katherine Davis Chapman Tillman* edited by Claudia Tate.[10]

Katherine Davis Chapman was born in Mound City, Illinois, in 1870; attended high school in Yanktown, South Dakota; and received additional education at the State University of Louisville in Kentucky and Wilberforce University. She married the Reverend George M. Tillman, an AME pastor in the western United States, and in 1910, they and their two-year-old adopted daughter, Dorothy, were living in Los Angeles. For two years prior to her death in 1923, she served as editor of the AME's *Women's Missionary Recorder*.[11]

Gertrude E. H. Bustill was born in Philadelphia on July 3, 1855. Her well-to-do family traced its lineage to a baker who supplied food to General George Washington and his troops. After her mother died, her father encouraged her love of reading, and she attended public school as well as the Institute for Colored Youth. She delivered a grammar school commencement speech, "Influence," that caught the attention of Henry McNeal Turner, and he published it in *The Christian Recorder* when she was just sixteen. During the 1870s she taught school and wrote for various periodicals, including some published by the AME denomination. After marrying Dr. Nathan F. Mossell in 1883, she withdrew from teaching and journalism to raise her two daughters but returned to journalism late in the decade, publishing in *The Colored American, Our Women and Children*, and *Ringwood's Afro-American Journal of Fashion*, among others. Her work also appeared in white periodicals including *The Philadelphia Times, The Philadelphia Inquirer*, and *The Philadelphia Press* as well as *The Ladies' Home Journal*. Like many Black women of her era, she was involved in the women's club movement and other organizations of racial uplift. Gertrude Mossell died on January 21, 1948, two years after her husband.[12]

Mossell's historical/biographical writings on Black women poets display a style of curation reminiscent of scrapbooking.[13] In revising the piece, Mossell both accrues new material—presumably clipped from the pages of the Black press—and excises references to some poets and poems included in earlier versions. The change from *Colored* to *Afro-American* in the essay's title may have constituted Mossell's response to "The New Race Name, Afro-American," an article in the January 12, 1893, issue of *The Christian Recorder*. Other changes included the addition of two names, Flora Batson and "Madame Jones," in the paragraph on well-known female singers and correction of "Charlotte Foster" to "Charlotte Forten" in the section on the antislavery movement. Mossell's discussion of H. Cordelia Ray includes two poems, "Sunset Picture" and "In Memoriam," the latter of which had just appeared. In addition, Mossell revised her description of Benjamin F. Lee, the husband of Mary Elizabeth Ashe Lee, from "ex-President of Wilberforce" to "Bishop" and added a lengthy excerpt from Lee's poem "Afmerica," which had appeared in the July 1885 issue of the *Review*. However, in the book version, Mossell neglected to revise her words regarding Mrs. M. E. Lambert, who "scarce needs an introduction to the readers of the *Review*."[14]

The final and most significant difference between the two versions of the essay is in their conclusions. The earlier version concludes with Esta Garnet's "A Prayer," taken from *The New York Freeman*, and Mossell's explanation, borrowed from Scripture (I Kings 10:7), "We give the latter [poem], and with it conclude our paper, with the single word, 'The half has not been told'" (67)—perhaps an indication that she intended to continue adding new material or that space considerations had forced her to cut short her essay. Whatever the case, the book version features ten additional pages of material beginning with the introduction of Josephine Heard and including poems Mossell culled from the pages of the *Review*, *The Christian Recorder*, *Ringwood's Afro-American Journal of Fashion*, and other publications.

Bentley's "The Women of Our Race Worthy of Imitation" (April 1890) mentions some of the same women listed in Mossell's *Review*

FIGURE 2.1. MRS. JULIA A. GAINES. FROM THE NEW YORK PUBLIC LIBRARY DIGITAL COLLECTIONS.

FIGURE 2.2. MRS. MARY L. ARNETT. FROM THE NEW YORK PUBLIC LIBRARY DIGITAL COLLECTIONS.

article but features women associated with the AME denomination—many the wives of ministers, bishops, or affiliates of Wilberforce University. According to Bentley, these women are "renowned for giving prudent advice in difficulties" and "endowed with intellectual powers as well as physical endurance"; their "literary attainments shine and charm society," and their "noble acts and deeds are lasting footprints on the sands of time" (473). Bentley's listing opens with Eliza J. Payne, second wife of Bishop Daniel A. Payne, the original president of Wilberforce, and E. Marie Shorter, whose husband, Bishop James A. Shorter, was a close associate of Payne.[15] Bentley next honors four more bishops' wives: Eliza Ann Turner, wife of Henry McNeal Turner; Julia A. Gaines, wife of Wesley John Gaines; Mary Louise Arnett, wife of Benjamin Williams Arnett; and Laura B. Greene, wife of Sherman Lawrence Greene. From here, Bentley moves on to praise Fanny Jackson Coppin, principal of Philadelphia's Institute for Colored Youth; Lucy C. Laney, principal of the Haines Institute in Augusta, Georgia; writer Lucretia H. Coleman; Fredericka Jones, principal at Paul Quinn College; Harper; Heard; Earle; activist and educator Hallie Q. Brown; singer Madame Selika; Lee; and

FIGURE 2.3. MRS. MARY ELIZABETH ASHE LEE. FROM THE NEW YORK PUBLIC LIBRARY DIGITAL COLLECTIONS.

FIGURE 2.4. MRS. MARY A. CAMPBELL. FROM THE NEW YORK PUBLIC LIBRARY DIGITAL COLLECTIONS.

Mary A. Campbell, president of the AME Church's Women's Mite Missionary Society.[16] Bentley concludes, "May we young women so fashion our lives after these model women that when the future historian shall portray in glaring letters the history of the Afro-American women, our names may be found in letters of gold" (477).

Upshaw's short essay praising "The Women of the A.M.E. Church" (January 1896) repeats some of the names noted by Mossell and Bentley, occasionally using nicknames to add a touch of familiarity. But Upshaw stretches back further in church history to note that in 1759, the "first black person baptized by John Wesley" was a woman who became a leader in Christian education in the West Indies (349) and to recognize Sarah Allen, whose husband, Richard Allen, founded the AME denomination. Moving forward to her contemporaries, Upshaw cites Anna Baltimore, a "pioneer mother" of the West and "Mrs. Dr. Robertson" (351). Upshaw expands the list of women singers and musicians to include Madam Dougan, Mattie Cheeks, J. Carrie Thomas, Mrs. Hamilton, Ida M. Yeocum, Lucy W. Church, Lulu Armstrong, Mary L. Gaines, and Willie Turner Gussie Haines (351). She also suggests how a history of AME churchwomen might be broadened to encompass "teachers in our Sabbath schools, day schools, colleges and universities" (352).[17] Upshaw concludes by admonishing her young women readers, "Your future happiness depends much on how well you have been trained by your parents and how well you have improved your opportunities" (352), taking her article into the category of advice column.[18]

Tillman's twenty-three-page essay, "Afro-American Women and Their Work" (April 1895), further broadens the focus on African American women while subtly challenging some prevailing class and gender norms. As Tate notes in her collection of Tillman's works, this essay's conclusion deploys a "discursive posture" used frequently by other African American women writers of the era by insisting that woman's most important work is in the home.[19] Indeed, Tillman opens by declaring that Eve serves as a "helpmeet" to Adam in the Garden of Eden and that woman's "mission in this world" is to "aid man in all of his stupendous undertakings" (477). However, Tillman then undercuts that position by establishing women's capabilities outside the home and under their own aegis.

Tillman begins her assault on traditional views of women's roles by asserting, "Since Christ was once cradled upon a woman's breast, there is no crown too royal for woman's brow" (478). For most of history, women "lived in a state of degradation, unappreciated, misunderstood and scorned as being as inferior to man as the rays of the candle are to the beams of the noonday sun" (478). Tillman cleverly links the rise of womanhood to the emergence of the Judeo-Christian heritage, observing that Christianity "taught man the true worth and ability of women" (478). She points to Miriam's role as a prophet in the Old Testament as well as Deborah's status as a judge over the Israelites, closing the paragraph by averring, "Christianity is emphatically the friend of women" (478).

Having brought her readers this far, Tillman dismisses earlier views that regarded women "either as a toy created for man's gratification, or as a slave doomed to an endless servitude" (478). She next makes the startling claim that under paganism and into medieval times, "immoral women fared better than those who were virtuous" (478), a sharp contrast with the "days of the busy honored lives of the mothers and daughters of the Nineteenth Century" (478). She then returns to the rhetorical posture with which she began: "All the privileges that woman enjoys to-day are gifts from Christianity"; "above all else," women ought to "spread the Gospel of Christ from shore to shore" (479).

But Tillman was not finished. She goes on to reveal the "motive" behind her essay: answering an unnamed Black editor's recent question, "What Have the Women of the Race Done for Its Elevation Anyway?" (implying that they had done nothing).[20] Tillman's response, featuring "interesting facts which cannot be disproved" (479), begins by tracing the deeds of African American women under slavery (479–84). She then catalogs race women's more modern contributions in the arenas of religion (485–87), education (487–90), art (490–97), and the home (497–99).

Opening the section on "The Religious World," Tillman ponders, "What would be the condition of the churches of all races and denominations, if the women were to withdraw their moral and financial support?" (485). In many churches, women raise funds to clothe the pastor and his family, prepare meals for the pastor, raise money to erect or renovate church buildings, and serve as missionaries and evangelists (486). Tillman's words reminded male clergy of the degree to which the generosity of their female parishioners was integral to the success of local ministries as well of the larger denomination.

In her section on "Educational Lines," Tillman speaks in the "broadest sense," defining the category to include "business women" (487)—those who own "first-class boarding houses," caterers, street vendors, laundresses, seamstresses, hairdressers, dealers in ice, dairy farmers, periodical canvassers, clerks, barbers, and merchandisers. The section also encompasses women who form co-ops for establishing banks, schools, and stores. With this shift in focus, Tillman moves beyond women of elite status to include Black women with varying levels of education and across the socioeconomic spectrum.

In "The World of Art," Tillman highlights art instructors and photographers, singers and music teachers, elocutionists, medical professionals, and finally educators and journalists. Again steering away from fields associated with W. E. B. Du Bois's "Talented Tenth," Tillman praises domestic servants: "Living in service is far happier than being yoked in an unhappy marriage, and a million times preferable to a life of shame!" (496). Traveling back up the socioeconomic ladder, Tillman notes the success of African American "society women," who "observe the same laws on etiquette" as their "Caucasian sisters" in terms of fashion, social visits, novel reading, card playing, and dancing (494)—a noteworthy list of pursuits in light of the fact that most AME churchmen considered them frivolous amusements.[21]

Concluding with "Afro-American Women in the Home," Tillman rues the fact that she cannot attest that the majority of Black homes are "what they should be" (495). However, she notes "great improvement" (498) and advises women to learn how to render a home "the happiest place on earth" (499). Women should wage "war against intemperance, against infidelity, against gambling in saloons or parlors, against bad literature and immorality of all kinds" (499). Moreover, Tillman reminds her readers, men and women alike, that as followers of Christ, they have a duty to serve as models for the rest of the world. Thus, while adopting rhetorical strategies designed to pacify her male readers, Tillman expands African American women's roles and displays an understanding of what would today be labeled the intersectionality of Black women's lives.[22]

These race histories widened the *Review*'s focus to encompass African American women as well as men. In this sense, these authors pioneered the crafting and popularizing of women's history as well as race history. They did the same in the fields of social work and sociology.

CHAPTER 3

Sociological Writings
Home, Family, Church

In the July 1896 issue of the *A.M.E. Church Review*, his first as editor, Hightower T. Kealing vowed to include matters "political, sociological, historical, archaeological, educational and philosophical" (175). In subsequent issues, he placed lead articles on these at the front of the journal, marking them in the table of contents with Roman numerals. The remainder of the publication contained a series of regular features under the titles "Miscellaneous," "Editorials," "Magazines and Reviews," "Our Book List," "All Opinions Department," and "Publisher's Department," not all of which appeared in every issue.

At the beginning of his second four-year term as editor, Kealing revised the format, grouping material into "Religious," "Educational," "Sociological," and "Scientific" departments beginning with the January 1901 "All Women Contributors" issue. Like most of these newly created departments, the sociology section primarily included excerpts from white journals. For example, in January 1901, an article from *The Saturday Evening Post* on the importance of saving money accompanied an editorial combining information from *The New York Evening Post* on the explosion in the Black population (from four million in the South at the close of the Civil War to ten million at the turn of the century) with an article from the AME Church's *Voice of Missions* advocating emigration to Liberia (263–67). Kealing

CONTENTS.

FRONTISPIECE.—Chromotype of Vicksburg, Miss., Church.
- I. ARCHITECTURE IN THE A. M. E. CHURCH.......... 103
- II. WHAT IS GOOD PREACHING..................... 109
- III. LEARNING TO BE MEN, By A. B. Cooper........... 117
- IV. WOMEN IN SOCIETY............................ 123
- V. THE EDUCATION OF THE NEGRO, By Howard E. Young 129
- VI. NEGRO JOURNALISM, By Willis T. Menard.......... 137
- VII. SHALL THE NEGRO LEAVE THE SOUTH, By C. T. Shaffer.. 143
- VIII. THE PROBLEM OF WORK, By W. E. Burghardt Du Bois 149

WOMEN—To Make a Happy Home—Woman: "The Arbiter of Praise or Blame"—Woman's Youth—Woman and the Republic..................... 170

SOCIOLOGICAL—Things we Don't Outgrow—Jamaica; Its People and Their Religion—Interesting Facts Concerning Public Men—A Peep into the British Museum, the World's School House—Sanitation and Sociology............................ 174

RELIGIOUS—Tell the Lord—The Census of India—How Ministers' Sons Turn Out—History of a Noted Hymn—Notes from South Africa........ 182

SCIENTIFIC—Ancient Beds—The Art of Getting to Sleep—Oysters as Food—Radium as a Cancer Cure 191

MISCELLANEOUS—Rest—A British View of Lynching—Some Additions—Why Most Cooks Always Stir Their Batter One Way Only—The Fall of Jericho—Potter 196

EDITORIAL—Men Are to be Judged as Units—A Novel Proposition—The Coming of the Nation's Saviors—Ephemera 208

FIGURE 3.1. *A.M.E. CHURCH REVIEW*, JANUARY 1904. COURTESY METHODIST COLLECTION, STYBERG LIBRARY, GARRETT EVANGELICAL THEOLOGICAL SEMINARY.

later added departments for both "Women" and "Business," with the former consisting largely of excerpts and reprints from other periodicals on topics addressing the supposed needs of women readers and the latter including the "Notes of Travel" column beginning in 1903 (see chapter 5).

Kealing's understanding of "sociological" contributions reflects the prevailing views of his era, which some historians of sociology have labeled "pre-sociology." Stephen Turner has argued that

"American sociology emerged out of a large universe of non-academic reform organizations," including such women-led organizations as the Woman's Christian Temperance Union (WCTU). Before the founding of the American Sociological Society in 1905, the boundaries between "social reform" and what would emerge as the academic field of sociology were far more fluid.[1] The work of American sociologist Mary Jo Deegan and Canadian professor of social work Lynn McDonald has done much to recuperate the early contributions of women both inside and outside the academy to the early history of sociology and social work. McDonald's work focuses primarily on early contributions made by white women social reformers of European descent working outside academic circles—for example, Harriet Taylor Mill (wife and writing collaborator of John Stuart Mill), Harriet Martineau, and Florence Nightingale.[2] Deegan's work on white and Black American women argues that they began with a concern for "the study of the home, women, children, and the family." However, as sociology institutionalized and its history became codified by white male academics, contributions from Black men and white and Black women were often ignored.[3] But as Patricia Hill Collins points out, "educated Black women intellectuals" exemplified "the tradition of merging intellectual work and activism." Likewise, Delores P. Aldridge identifies women such as Anna Julia Cooper and Ida B. Wells-Barnett as practitioners of "engaged-sociology" in the late nineteenth and early twentieth centuries.[4] Fannie Barrier Williams, who contributed three sociological essays to the *Review* between 1897 and 1913, subsequently was largely obscured as "a significant community leader, intellectual, [and] sociologist" until the 1980s saw an "explosion in scholarship on African American women."[5]

That scholarship has helped to bring about a broader definition of *sociology*.[6] Modifying the work of German sociologist Dirk Kasler, Deegan establishes that women can be identified as early sociologists if they (1) occupied a chair of sociology and/or taught sociology; (2) held membership in a sociological society; (3) authored or coauthored sociological articles or textbooks; (4) self-defined as sociologists; or (5) were seen by others as sociologists. Deegan found fifty-one "founding sisters" of sociology who met at least one of these criteria.[7]

This chapter teases out the early histories of these overlapping sociological fields before turning to *Review* contributors' writings in those areas, while the following chapter examines writings targeting larger societal reform initiatives.

The institutional roots of sociology as an academic discipline can be traced to the University of Chicago's 1892 creation of a graduate department in sociology, which initially excluded women. However, "applied sociology," or what some refer to as the fledging field of social work, attracted women's contributions from its earliest days. Issues such as temperance, family instability, education, suffrage, aging, and a host of other societal ills led women individually as well as collectively to advocate for and establish organizations such as the WCTU and the National Woman Suffrage Association as well as institutions such as schools, orphanages, reformatories, and homes for the aged. And women—some of whom were recognized in their day as vital participants in the emerging fields of sociology and social reform work—contributed articles on these topics to the *Review*. By printing these articles, Kealing granted cultural authority and recognition to the sociologists, social workers, criminologists, and reformers who authored the works.

Male Editors and Female Contributors

Kealing's predecessors at the helm of the *Review* had differing views on women's standing in the church and society as well as opinions about the appropriate genres and topics for women contributors to pursue. The *Review*'s first editor, Benjamin T. Tanner, took a conservative position regarding many women's issues, among them ordination, divorce laws, and suffrage, arguing that AME churchmen would take care of women's interests. Nonetheless, Tanner strongly advocated women's education, possibly because his mother, although very intelligent, had been denied formal learning opportunities. Indeed, one of Tanner's daughters, Hallie, earned a degree from the Women's Medical College of Philadelphia.[8]

Tanner's successor, Levi J. Coppin, adopted a more liberal approach to the roles of women, particularly in terms of their contributions to the quarterly. By the time he took over as editor in 1888, he had been married for nearly seven years to Fanny Jackson Coppin, principal of Philadelphia's Institute for Colored Youth, who was fifteen years his senior. Fanny Coppin had initiated *The Christian Recorder*'s "Woman's Department," in which she "urged women to look to nontraditional fields, to strive to be financially independent of men, and to consider opening their own businesses." At the time of their marriage, Levi requested that she give up her position and join him at his pastorate in Baltimore, but Fanny refused, and the two lived apart for several years. Under Levi Coppin's stewardship, the *Review*'s offerings included short stories and serialized fiction, most of which was contributed by women, as well as scientific writings.[9]

In general, these editors' views reflected prevailing nineteenth-century ideas regarding "separate spheres" and "true womanhood": the ideal woman was the queen of her home and a helpmeet to her husband. She was responsible for the moral education of her children and was devoted to piety, purity, submission, and domesticity.[10] Male contributors, too, tended to circumscribe women's roles. For example, C. Hatfield Dickerson's "Woman Suffrage" (October 1887) opposed the extension of the franchise, and James H. A. Johnson believed that "Woman's Exalted Station" (April 1892) was limited to the home sphere. Women contributors, however, imagined a more capacious role for themselves, couching it within a rhetorical posture I call "pious feminism," though they would not have applied the term *feminism* to their writing and activism. Their contributions were primarily "didactic" in nature—that is, "intended primarily to teach rather than to entertain."[11] Therefore, *pious feminism* can serve as shorthand for views that embraced a commitment to the racial uplift of Black women (feminism) but did so within the boundaries of religious faith (pious).

At first glance the concept of pious feminism may seem problematic. While Collins connects Cooper, Frances Ellen Watkins Harper, and Wells-Barnett to early expressions of "Black feminist thought," other Black women scholars disagree with this assessment. Aldridge prefers to designate Cooper and Wells-Barnett as "early 'engaged' social theorists" and chronicles the scholarly disputes arising from applying the term *feminist* to these Black women, particularly the argument that feminism is a white women's ideology and movement. However, as Collins states, "Rather than developing definitions and arguing over naming Practices—for example, whether this thought should be called Black feminism, womanism, Afrocentric Feminism, Africana womanism, and the like—a more useful approach lies in revising the reasons why black feminist thought exists at all."[12]

Women in the Home and Church

The views expressed by women writers often converged with those expressed by the male contributors, particularly in the early years of the *Review*'s publication. Women contributors were frequently the wives of church ministers and bishops, so this alignment is not terribly surprising. Yet some of these wives argued for expanded roles within the framework of pious feminism. For example, Mary Elizabeth Ashe Lee, whose husband, the Reverend Benjamin F. Lee, eventually became a bishop, opened "The Home-Maker" (July 1891), by asserting "I believe in woman's rights. She should be or do whatever God has called and fitted her to be and do" (63). She avows the importance of women's temperance reform work and opines that "woman's suffrage is a good thing" (63). Acknowledging the view that voting might render women "coarse and rough," she counters that instead, women "might reform the manner of conducting the polls" (64), thereby rendering a service to the nation. However, she cautions that domestic duties must remain women's primary responsibility: "No greater calamity could happen than for a woman to neglect her home and children" (64).

Lee next recounts the recent fiftieth birthday celebration of a friend. Although she does not name the woman, the details reveal that she was Sarah Elizabeth Miller Tanner, the wife of Benjamin Tanner, who was born on May 18, 1840.[13] Lee's friend is the "queen" of her home, and the "works of her life" as a wife and mother constitute "a grand success," with a son who was an artist, a daughter who married an attorney, and another daughter who had earned a medical degree (64). Though trained as a teacher and "full of aspirations" for "the uplifting of her people" (64), this friend married and gave up her teaching aspirations to support her husband's "life's work" (64). Because the responsibilities of a homemaker are "so many and so heavy" that many young women may become discouraged, Lee cites her friend to offer reassurance that they too will see the rewards in due time (65). In closing, Lee opines that the "unselfish efforts of our mothers" are necessary for the race to "measure up equally with the Anglo-Americans" (66).

If the rank-and-file women of the race were expected to embrace homemaking as their primary aspiration in life, much greater demands were placed on the wives of ministers and bishops. In "Woman's Work and Influence in Home and Church" (July 1906), Mrs. G. E. Taylor, whose husband was the Reverend G. E. Taylor, editor of *The Southern Christian Recorder*, harshly criticizes wives, particularly ministers' wives, who scold and nag their husbands (23).[14] However, she also addresses the delicate issue of ministerial infidelity, observing that the "question of purity of the pulpit would largely be solved, if more of the wives possessed that sweetness of disposition which their husbands once thought they had" (23). Moreover, she notes that since a "complete union" between spouses means a "spiritual, a mental and a physical mating" and "the physical mating is" often "not what it should be," leading to discord. She advises mothers to teach both sons and daughters the expectations of married union and thus avoid the "divorce evil" (23–24) and its impact on children. Though she accuses some women of abandoning motherly care and the education of their children, she blames such actions on "worthless" men who shirk their responsibility to support their families and thus compel women to labor outside the home (21). Like other contributors to the *Review*, Taylor contends that "no race ever rises higher than its women," reminding women readers that "destiny . . . is in your hands" (24).[15]

"The Minister's Wife" (April 1913), written by Mary A. Handy, the wife of Bishop James A. Handy and the president of the Women's Parent Mite Missionary Society, a group of northern AME churchwomen formed in 1874, largely agrees with Taylor.[16] Handy, however, eschews sexual topics and confines herself to the positive contributions the minister's wife should make to her home, the church, and the community. Concurring with the author of a recent editorial in a church publication, Handy believes that just as a man must receive a call to the ministry, "the woman he would make his wife" should feel called to serve her husband's ministry (337). The minister is therefore responsible for choosing a wife wisely: "many failures in the Ministry may be traced to indiscretion in choosing a companion" (337). Because ministers' salaries are often insufficient and their health compromised by overwork, Handy urges wives and family members to set aside money for the purchase of a house that will provide "peace and comfort" in retirement (338), thus making women financial as well as physical caretakers.

Handy's article is immediately followed by two articles titled "Women as Helpers of the Ministers in the Spiritual and Social Activities of the Church." The first was submitted by Rosina Palmer Chappelle, the second wife of the Reverend William D. Chappelle, who served as president of Allen University and secretary-treasurer of the AME Sunday School Union and who was elected a bishop in

FIGURE 3.2. MRS. MARY A. HANDY. FROM THE NEW YORK PUBLIC LIBRARY DIGITAL COLLECTIONS.

1912. The couple's April 24, 1900, nuptials received prominent notice in *The Christian Recorder*, and Rosina Chappelle later became an officer in the Woman's Home and Foreign Missionary Society.[17]

Chappelle's article focuses on rank-and-file churchwomen, stressing how they can assist ministers by praying and leading during club and prayer group meetings and by reaching out to welcome less fortunate members of the congregation as fellow Christians and to "build up the membership of the church" (339–40). Chappelle evidently practiced what she preached, prompting her husband to observe that she "rendered great assistance in his rise to prominence in the AME Church."[18]

The second article, by Katherine Davis Tillman, begins delineating women's contributions to the Judeo-Christian heritage, citing, among others, Eve, Miriam, Esther, Abigail, and the Widow of Zarephath from the Old Testament and Jesus's mother Mary, Mary Magdalene, and various additional New Testament women. Moving to the present, Tillman alleges that "men who have no heart interest in the welfare of the Church contribute liberally in its support" as a consequence of the influence of their pious wives (342). She praises women evangelists who are "winning thousands" to the church as well as the deaconesses who visit community members in their homes and members of women's societies (342).[19] Women who participate in church services might prove to be "spiritual magnets," drawing visitors and strangers into the community, a "blessed work" no matter how "and by whom it may be done" (342). In keeping with the denomination's conservative position regarding women and ministry, Tillman ends by reiterating that women are particularly suited to all these duties in the church by virtue of their role as "home makers of the centuries" (343).

In the wake of World War I, when women played active roles both in industry and in the war effort, some women writers reconsidered women's relationship to home and family. In "What of the Children?" (July 1922), Josephine J. Turpin Washington offered a sociological analysis of the era's rapid cultural changes. According to Washington, the need for women to move into jobs normally occupied by men "accelerated the movement on behalf of equal rights," resulting in a "very open field" for women in education and the professions (8). Moreover, women's ongoing desire to remain employed outside the home could not be explained by the financial benefits alone but rather reflected their feeling that they "were doing something really worth while" (9)

She then observes, "Ah, there's the rub," ruing the fact that work inside the home is no longer perceived as valuable (9). Washington chides the "childless married woman" with too much time on her hands as a consequence of the development of labor-saving devices and who becomes "money-mad" for entertainment and possessions (9). She fears that women will choose to remain childless and notes that the Roman Catholic Church teaches that married couples who refuse to have children cannot be truly pious. After bearing children, a woman "should pause long before turning her face away from her own fireside," since as the work of psychologist and educator G. Stanley Hall demonstrates, a woman's "highest duty" is in the education of her children (9). Washington also cites an observation from Dorothy Canfield Fisher, an educational reformer and social activist who supported women's rights, that couples who approach raising children as an opportunity "for unexpectedness, for sanity and laughter and health and pure joy," will be on the right track. Washington agrees: "If we place the child where he belongs in our hearts and lives, the rest"—women's relations to "the world's work," "civic claims," "society," and the church—will follow" (10). Washington concludes by making a bold, progressive claim for the passage of "mother pension laws" to ensure that women do not need to work outside the home. But that, she says, "is another story" (10).

While these contributors couched their sociological writings comfortably within the accepted framework of their roles as Christian wives, mothers, and homemakers, others imagined a more capacious realm for women in the public sphere, becoming leaders in social reform movements. In particular, access to higher education allowed these women to embrace work now regarded as part of the emerging field of sociology.

CHAPTER 4

Sociological Writings
Suffrage, Temperance, Criminality, Prison Reform

The sociological writings related to social reform movements argue eloquently for expanded citizen rights for African American women. Within the confines of pious feminism, these contributors to the *A.M.E. Church Review* pushed back against the larger white culture's attempts to criminalize Black behavior and the carceral systems that punished Black bodies. As Brigitte Fielder and Jonathan Senchyne note, "Against the various and historical forms of physical violence, structural exclusion, and attempts at rhetorical erasure, the work of African American print culture often responds to such gaps and unanswered question, becoming itself a form of resistance and antithesis to black death."[1]

As her biographer, Wanda A. Hendricks, points out, pioneering Black sociologist Fannie Barrier Williams was "a mixed-race educated elitist" well known in her day as a clubwoman, reformer, and journalist who published dozens of articles in major periodicals.[2] Scholar Brittney C. Cooper describes Williams's 1893 Chicago World's Fair address as among the first calls "for a systematic study of Black women as a separate and distinct category among African Americans."[3] Although Williams, a Unitarian, was not a member of the AME Church, her social reform work featured prominently in the *Review*.[4]

In "The Awakening of Women" (April 1897), Williams observes that "the most aggressive forces in the reform movements of the day" originate not from established institutions such as churches and schools but rather from urban voluntary associations (392). Using her hometown as a case study, she points to Chicago's Civic Federation, "made up of the best men and women of all parties and interests," as well as the city's women's clubs, which provided services not offered by schools, churches, or local governments (393). Williams's friend Jane Addams at Hull House and other women who go into the slum districts give "new value to womanly worth" (394). Assessing class differences, she argues that "the lower half" has less need for money or institutions than for "a sense of relationship and fellowship with the upper half" (394), a phenomenon she labels socialty and from which both sets of women benefit. Williams further touts the need for "study and preparation" before undertaking the work of social reform. Understanding that social reform that provides a "remedy" is not a "cure," she advocates "special intelligence" that gets at the root causes of "disease and poverty" (398). As Mary Jo Deegan convincingly demonstrates, Williams was committed to empirically driven reform work.[5]

"Women in Society" (October 1903), was written by Lucy Williams Hubert, the wife of the Reverend Ellwood G. Hubert of Darby, Pennsylvania. Lucy E. Williams was born on March 20, 1864, in Morton, Pennsylvania; married Hubert on October 18, 1888; and served as president of the Mite Missionary Society of the Bethel AME Church in York, Pennsylvania, in 1901. In 1898, she published *Hints on the Care of Children*, a book offering advice to Black mothers, and in November 1902, she gave an address at a "Women's Day at Siloam" event that likely provided the basis for her *Review* article.[6]

Hubert opens the article by declaring that as a result of nineteenth-century advancements, women are "in nearly all respects, the equals of men" (122). The denominations that now ordain women include the Universalists, Unitarians, Congregationalists, and some branches of the Baptist and Methodist churches (although the AME

Figure 4.1. Lucy E. Hubert. Courtesy the Library Company of Philadelphia Reading Room.

Church did not). Using data from the 1900 US Census, she points out that women have entered virtually every field, including those requiring higher education (such as law, medicine, and the church) as well as those requiring manual labor (blacksmithing, butchery, and wood masonry) (122–23). But women have made more important contributions "to society," among them "scientific temperance instruction" and the Woman's Christian Temperance Union (124). She also praises Frances Joseph's prison reform work in New Orleans, New York City's Colored Orphan Asylum, Boston's Watch and Ward Society, and the many reform efforts spearheaded by Frances Ellen Watkins Harper and Fanny Jackson Coppin (125–27). In closing, Hubert nods to the conventional wisdom regarding the importance of home duties by mentioning a woman's epitaph that reads, "She always made home happy," before inserting a poem that begins with a reference to the Gospel of John, 4:35: "Truly the fields are white for the harvest" (127). Thus, Hubert melds pious feminism with data-driven analysis.

Selena C. Gaines Dickerson echoed Hubert's sentiments a dozen years later in "The Responsibilities and Duties of the Women of the Twentieth Century" (October 1915). Dickerson had been a teacher in the public schools of Xenia, Ohio, since the turn of the century; was a founding member and local and national official of the National Grand Chapter of the Order of Eastern Star; frequently addressed local, state, and national conventions; and was a member of Xenia's Black Twentieth Century Club. Her article for the *Review*, contributed when Dickerson was in her forties, demonstrates both her erudition and her wide life experiences.[7]

In words suggestive of the emerging Social Gospel movement, Dickerson argues that "Christian work is social" (108). Such views likely resonated with *Review* editor Reverdy C. Ransom, known for his embrace of Social Gospel movement.[8] Suggesting that success depends on associations, reading material, loved ones, and even diet, she pronounces one's lifework a "spiritual product" regardless of religious affiliation, since "no church has a monopoly on salvation" (109–10). In keeping with pious feminism, she writes that "mothers must not neglect their children," she also argues that they must not neglect themselves (109). Women's work—whether in the home, in church, in the community, or for pay—is "to serve": to "mold character, teach righteousness, disseminate peace," and spread "Christian charity" (110).

Suffrage

The question of women's suffrage arose with some frequency in the *Review*. Some women contributors rejoiced over the possibility of gaining long-denied political rights, while others proved more skeptical. In "Woman Suffrage" (July 1910), Effie B. Carter took the same tack as many of the *Review*'s male contributors, arguing against granting women the right to vote. Carter was a widowed mixed-race woman living in Xenia, Ohio, and studying at Wilberforce University, and her article appears to be based on the valedictory speech she delivered at Wilberforce's July 1910 commencement. Carter later served as recording secretary for the Ohio Conference Branch of the Woman's Mite Missionary Society.[9]

Carter begins with what she calls "the American doctrine of rights" (43). Although men and women are "alike" in some ways, the right to vote should be based not on their "equality" but on some other qualification—suffrage for American men requires them to pay taxes, perform military service, or meet other criteria (49). Thus, she argues, women must secure their right to vote "out of history, out of providential preparations and causes, out of the concessions of custom, out of debated reasons of public benefit" (50). But Carter does not believe that women benefit from enfranchisement. She quotes former president Theodore Roosevelt, who saw no "special improvement in the position of women" in Idaho, Colorado, Utah, and Wyoming, which already allowed women to vote (51). Moreover, women have a "higher, finer nature" that would be contaminated were they to "come down to competition with men" in the political arena (51–52). Espousing the separate spheres gender ideology, Carter argues that women should occupy the "higher" realms—the home, the church, social life, literature, and art—and that "the vast majority of women will long continue to remain content in the sphere they now occupy" (52–53). Her use of the singular *sphere* indicates her view that the home is the proper domain of women: it is an "empire" where they "can reign supreme" and "rule the world" through "influence unswayed by the faintest echo of partisan strife and political corruption" (53).

Fannie Barrier Williams's second *Review* article, "Suffrage in Illinois" (October 1913), appeared shortly after that state granted women the right to vote. Writing just three years after Carter, Williams crows, "One by one the old hard and fast theories as to 'Woman's sphere' are giving way to newer and more progressive ideals" (122). Williams speculates about how Black women voters might influence politics nationwide, pointing out that "most white people" remain unaware that many African American women earn college degrees, work, and pay taxes (122–23). Despite the prevailing system of racism and taxation without representation, Black women have registered notable accomplishments in education, philanthropy, and forming benevolent organizations, demonstrating their engagement in great "public questions" (123). Because Black men do not always vote in ways likely to benefit women, Black women's suffrage can "force open" the "doors of opportunity" that currently remain closed (123).

Williams argues that the franchise gives women greater leverage in reversing unjust measures such as Chicago laws a that forbid African American youth from entering business colleges, allow dependent Black girls to be segregated in underfunded institutions, and prohibit white women from employment in "questionable" houses in the red-light district but allow African American women to engage in such work (123–24). She urges Black women to form groups to study the areas of concern for women and children rather than simply voting in tandem with African American men: "We certainly cannot afford to follow the examples of some of the colored patriots who learn their politics in saloons and policy shops" (124). The franchise means that "for the first time in our history, colored women will be able to compel respect for themselves" (124).

With the ratification of the Nineteenth Amendment on the horizon, the editorial position of the *Review* appears to have shifted rather significantly. "Colored Women and the Suffrage" (April 1918), was written by George W. Forbes, who took charge of the *Review*'s editorial duties when Ransom was traveling. Forbes took the opportunity to criticize Southerners' opposition to women's suffrage on the grounds that it would include African American women. In the wake of the April 1920 ratification of the Nineteenth Amendment, the *Review* published an October 1920 editorial, "At Last Woman Suffrage—a Son's Gift to Mother," pointing out that the amendment went into effect only after Harry T. Burns, the youngest member of the Tennessee legislature, broke a deadlock by casting his vote in favor after receiving a letter from his mother urging him to do so (91).

The "Color Question"

While most of the women whose work was published in the *Review* were Black, the contributions of white reformers occasionally appeared, as was the case with Caroline Hollingsworth Pemberton's "Experiences and Observations in the Black Belt, amid the 'Souls of Black Folk'" (July 1904). Pemberton was a member of a prominent Pennsylvania Quaker family, the daughter of Henry Pemberton, a scholar and scientist who wrote *The Path of Evolution Through Ancient Thought and Modern Science*, and Caroline Towne Hollingsworth Pemberton. After spending time in the household of her uncle, Confederate general John C. Pemberton, Caroline Pemberton became critical of the treatment of southern Black citizens and wrote two novels, *Your Little Brother James* (1896) and *Stephen the Black* (1899). She subsequently turned to socialism, writing and speaking on behalf of party causes through at least 1904. Contemporary periodicals also considered her a sociologist.[10]

Pemberton's *Review* article narrates some of her experiences traveling in the South. She is surprised when an apparently "white woman" greets her at the door of Booker T. Washington's home and further surprised when the woman declares that she is Black (63). Pemberton writes scathingly of the mortgage system and peonage system that consistently robbed Black citizens of the products of their labors, agreeing with a farmer's wife that "the white people live off the colored people" (64). When she travels with Black schoolteachers, one explains that she cannot sit with Pemberton and instead must ride in the Jim Crow car; on another occasion, a lighter-skinned teacher sits with Pemberton, but when they reach their destination, they mistakenly enter the Colored waiting room, raising the ire of the white men who also disembark (65). "So much for race mixture in the South," she concludes (65). Pemberton's writing reveals her belief in the absurdity of racial designation based on scientific racism and social Darwinism, which, as Aldon D. Morris demonstrates, formed the nucleus of most theoretical work

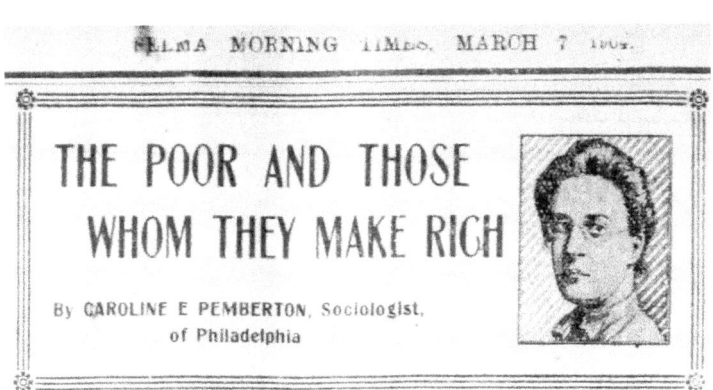

FIGURE 4.2. CAROLINE HOLLINGSWORTH PEMBERTON. COURTESY NEWSPAPERS.COM.

emerging from academic sociology departments, particularly at the University of Chicago.[11]

Emma Azalia Hackley, a Black woman raised in Detroit, Michigan, explained to readers "How the Color Question Looks to an American in France" (January 1907). An excellent student and accomplished musician, Hackley earned a bachelor's degree in music from the University of Denver and later spent several years traveling outside the United States and introducing listeners to African American folk music.[12]

During her nine months in France, she did not exchange "one word with a colored resident of Paris." Rather, her article presents her observations of the treatment of African Americans living there (210). The French call all persons of darker complexion *negro* whether they hail from India, Egypt, Ethiopia, or the United States (211). She maintains that the French "despise black people," citing newspaper coverage of visiting dignitaries from India and Africa that belittle and caricature both these visitors and African Americans living in France (211, 215). Hackley observes that African Americans seldom congregate together—the men prefer the company of white Frenchwomen—unlike the "Black French" or the West Indians, whom she pronounces "rather clannish" for eschewing the companionship of others (212). Likewise, white Americans do not mingle with African Americans (214). Although the French claim that skin color is no barrier in France, pointing to the success of father and son Alexandre Dumas, she claims that French people "will laugh in the faces of Negroes on the street" and that French aristocrats take a very unfavorable view of intermarriage (213). Hackley finds it strange that the English in France prove more cordial to African Americans than do the French (214), a phenomenon she attributes in part to French ignorance about the United States, most French, she states, believe all African Americans live in the South (215). Hackley concludes with an assertion of race pride: despite the supposed beauty of "Black-French women in Paris," she finds the "average colored American woman" far more attractive (215).

Leonora Beck Ellis contributed a two-part article, "The Southern Negro as a Property-Owner" (January and April 1908), that ran with a rare prefatory editorial note. Kealing explained that the piece had originally appeared in *Tom Watson's Magazine*, a Georgia-based Populist Party publication.[13] Kealing made an exception to his policy of printing only original pieces because he found the author's evidence most compelling and supportive of the efforts of Black farmers and property owners. Ellis was already recognized as a pioneering sociologist and had published on child labor in cotton mills in the *American Journal of Sociology*, the flagship journal of the University of Chicago's sociology program. Ellis's work, like that of most early women sociologists, took an empirical approach that contrasted with male sociologists' preference for theoretical work that reinforced scientific racism.[14]

Ellis's article establishes her empirical approach by citing statistics published by the Department of Labor (January 1908, 235). She explains that she chose Georgia for her case study because of its geographic size, substantial Black population, and rural nature: Georgia's African Americans owned more than a million acres of land (237–38). A recent conference of the state's African American farmers had drawn two hundred attendees, all of whom owned land

FIGURE 4.3. LEONORA BECK ELLIS, 1893. COURTESY WIKIPEDIA COMMONS.

and many of whom were comparatively wealthy, including one person who was worth $50,000 (240).

Ellis subsequently drills down to provide county-level statistics. She compares Black landowning in two resource-rich coastal counties, Chatham (which includes Savannah) and Liberty, which have very different settlement histories, with landownership in Appling, an inland county with poor soil (April 1908, 314–16). She finds that African Americans have bought up land at higher rates than whites but own smaller parcels, a fact that she believes "augurs well" because they can work the land without hiring additional labor and can support themselves and their families, albeit meagerly (318–19). She also notes that African Americans now own 29 percent of all city property (320). She concludes, "The Negro with a home is almost sure to stand for law, order and civic faithfulness," an assessment that *Review* readers would have celebrated.

The migration of African Americans out of the rural South to Northern cities created a host of sociological problems in the opening decade of the twentieth century. While most *Review* articles highlighted Black men's labor conditions, Sarah Willie Layten's "A

Northern Phase of a Southern Problem" (March 1910) focused on young girls. Layten served as president of the women's auxiliary of the National Baptist Convention and was involved with several other Afro-Protestant civic and social organizations, including the National Association of Colored Women and the National Urban League, making her a formidable figure both nationally and in her home city, Philadelphia. After receiving a degree from Lemoyne College, Layten completed graduate courses in sociology at Temple University and in social work through the University of Pennsylvania. In 1943, *The Chicago Tribune* pronounced her "a pioneer in social work."[15]

Written to solicit support for the National League for the Protection of Colored Women, a group headquartered in New York City with branches in Baltimore and Philadelphia, Layten's eleven-page lead article is prefaced by an editorial commentary in which Kealing notes that Layten's experience living in both the North and the South renders her "splendidly fitted" to write about the challenges of young women fleeing the "social plague" of life below the Mason-Dixon Line. The article opens with a snippet from a "Letter from a Southern girl in the North" advising her sister not to relocate until she receives word from her northern kin since "it is awful hard to get anything to do if you are black" (315). Layten observes that two kinds of women come north: those seeking education, who have the means to care for themselves, and those of little means, who seek employment and greater freedom. She decries the "harpies and procuresses" who take advantage of the latter group, often steering them into unsavory occupations (316). Layten praises the National League's founder, Frances Kellor, as a "modern type" with "college training in social problems" (316) and explains the organization's educational and social service work.[16] The league uses the press, churches, and community organizations to distribute literature urging women not to come north but provides those who ignore that advice with assistance in finding safe shelter, jobs, social connections, and wholesome entertainment (317–19).

But there are gaps in the system: more "matrons" are needed to guide the new arrivals and to combat the actions of "employment agents" who recruit girls to travel north, where they are vulnerable to exploitation (320). In an oblique dig at male sociologists, Layten declares, "Very little time is given to theory in this League. Work is needed and work is done" (324). She concludes with seven rules for young women considering a move to the North and urges them to write to the National League's New York office before embarking on the northward journey. Layten also advocates that the South's young women receive further education about the challenges and dangers of migration.

Temperance and Criminality

Both men and women contributors to the *Review* were concerned about the consumption of alcoholic beverages and its presumed link to criminal activity, which could leave Black women and children vulnerable to harm. The quarterly published ten male-authored feature articles on the subject of intemperance between July 1885 and the onset of Prohibition with the 1919 passage of the Eighteenth Amendment.[17] In addition, the *Review*'s Religious, Women, Sociological, and Editorial Departments teemed with discussions of the topic, although only eight appeared in lead articles with the subject in the article title.[18] Women contributed four major temperance articles during this period: Harper wrote two of them and coordinated an April 1891 symposium on the subject, while Rosetta E. Lawson authored the fourth.

Better known as a novelist, lecturer, abolitionist, journalist, and clubwoman, Harper taught at Union Seminary in Wilberforce, Ohio, and at a school in York, Pennsylvania. So sweeping was her influence on print culture that she was referred to as the "'journalistic mother' of the African American press," contributing articles to a wide range of periodicals, among them *The Provincial Freeman, Frederick Douglass'*

Paper, *The New York Independent*, *The Weekly Anglo African*, and *The Woman's Era*. Harper was affiliated with the Unitarian Church but also contributed to AME causes and publications.[19] In "The Woman's Christian Temperance Union and the Colored Woman" (January 1888), Harper opens with a vignette of a seemingly helpless woman watching her home ravaged by the evils of intemperance before shifting to the 1873 Woman's Crusade and women's antisaloon efforts (313).[20] Citing Victor Hugo's pronouncement of the nineteenth century as "woman's era," Harper identifies "twin evils": slavery and intemperance (313). She argues that immigrants who were "subjects" in their own lands earned "freedom" by coming to America and then proceeded to sway legislators against Prohibition (314). Harper narrates the formation of the Woman's Christian Temperance Union (WCTU) and the National Christian Temperance Union, which welcomed both white and Black members and in which Harper was currently serving as superintendent of work among African Americans in the North (314). Harper exhorts her readers to join the battle against "intoxicating drinks" in the home by teaching children to abhor alcohol as well as in the larger community, even if doing so results in scorn from fashionable society and white citizens who fears "social contact" with African Americans (316).

A year later, Harper published a follow-up article, "National Woman's Christian Temperance Union" (January 1889). In the preceding year, she had given "more than a hundred addresses" on behalf of the cause, sometimes receiving compensation for her travel expenses but never talking a "wage" for her labor (242). In spite of the "defeats of the past year," limited progress had occurred nearly a dozen states (242–45). According to an Illinois woman, "Mrs. Villa," some local Prohibition ordinances had succeeded but other efforts had been stymied by "liquor interests"—business owners who threatened to dismiss any employees whose wives and sisters supported the WCTU (243). Marylander "Mrs. Many" reported the formation of six WCTU chapters for Black women with a total of 158 members (244). Sarah D. Brown from St. Louis reported success in raising $360 to construct a home for children orphaned as a consequence of intemperance (245). Harper closes by praying for clarity of vision and more "blessed possibilities" in the coming year (245).

In April 1891, the *Review* featured a symposium on temperance, with contributions from Harper, Mary W. Howe, "Mrs. W. T. Anderson," and Ida B. Wells. Howe was "Principal of the Willston School (colored)" of Wilmington, North Carolina, and Anderson served as principal of the Normal College at the J. P. Campbell College in Vicksburg, Mississippi, where her husband was president.[21] As in her previous articles, Harper judges the "slavery of intemperance" far worse than the "American slavery" brought to an end by the Civil War (173): "the calamities which flow from alcohol" far exceed "those which come from war, pestilence and famine" (173). Continuing the martial metaphor, she urges readers to adopt a four-pronged approach to battling intemperance—"consecrate, educate, agitate, and legislate" (374)—that also positions temperance work as holy Christian work. Also in keeping with pious feminism, she suggests that education begin in the home (375). To agitate, Harper urges women to "clasp hands with the best women in the land, North and South" (375), and she advises women who can vote in local elections to vote as Christians against the liquor traffic; Black men should avoid adhering to party lines or factions or joining a "third party" (likely a reference to the Prohibition Party) but should use their "numerical strength," "moral power," and "spiritual influence" to battle against intemperance (375).

Howe identifies three issues as causing agitation in the United States: the "Indian Question, the Negro Problem and the Temperance Question" (375). In her view, temperance is the most important because it does not "partake of the idea of caste" but is rather "the great leveler," crushing people of all walks of life, and a kind of idol—the "Baal to which the nation bows" (376). She responds to the argument that the liquor trade provides the government with revenue for education by pointing out that it also requires the government to construct and operate asylums, hospitals, and prisons to house those damaged by intemperance (376). Howe notes a Chicago judge's contention that 95 percent of boys in reform schools are there because alcohol use either killed their parents or forced them to become criminals (377). She also cites a paper presented to the American Social Science Association that purports to find that 40 percent of drunkards have "inebriate ancestry" (377). Howe concludes by noting that women as well as men can become alcoholics (377).

Anderson's contribution declares intemperance "the greatest enemy of our time," snatching bread out of children's mouths (378). Asserting that intemperance has been a problem throughout human history, she claims that the outcomes of the Battle of Waterloo and the Revolutionary War resulted from leaders under the influence of alcohol (378). Moreover, members of "respectable society" who serve wine to guests are "giving them the dagger to take their own lives" (379). Anderson concludes by pronouncing temperance a "progressive" cause and by imagining a future in which grain and grape are never crushed and all distilleries are destroyed, thereby setting free weeping mothers and oppressed children (379).

Historian Mia Bay argues that "despite their familiarity with the racial theories of their era . . . African American women rarely dealt with them directly in a more extended way."[22] Wells's contribution to the temperance symposium represents one of the exceptions. Insisting that African Americans are no more intemperate than other races, she points to systemic problems of "poverty, ignorance, and consequent degradation" that render Black folks less able to "afford" this level of equality with other races (379). Wells believes that there is some truth in temperance activist Frances E. Willard's allegations that Black men sold their votes in the recent Prohibition campaign and that Black men frequent saloons while white men are too afraid to do so but argues that even when intoxicated, Black men rarely hurt anyone but each other (380). Farmers can waste a year of profit on intoxicating liquors and consequently remain in debt, while young Black men can enter the alcohol trade to earn money (380). Wells argues that schools need to adopt a "systematic course

FIGURE 4.4. ROSETTA E. LAWSON. FROM THE NEW YORK PUBLIC LIBRARY DIGITAL COLLECTIONS.

of instruction from an economic standpoint" that will educate students regarding the financial consequences of intemperance (381). She also urges the National Press Association to stress to its "million readers" the physical and financial impacts of intemperance and implores ministers to continue to preach temperance to their flocks. An "organized combination of all these agencies" will be needed to reverse the impacts of the liquor trade (381).

While the symposium focuses on the national problem created by the liquor trade, Lawson's "The Temperance Reform a World-Wide Movement" (January 1901) looks at the international scope of both the problem and the response. Born to a free Black mother in Virginia prior to the Civil War, Rosetta Evelyn Coakley was raised in Washington, DC. She completed a course through New York's Chautauqua Institution in 1884, and later that year married Jesse Lawson, a graduate of Howard University who became a lawyer, activist, and educator. In 1895, with her husband serving as an organizer for the Cotton States and International Exposition held in Atlanta, she helped to arrange the Atlanta Congress of Colored

Figure 4.5. Joseph Gaudet, from *He Leadeth Me*. Courtesy of HathiTrust Digital Library.

Women. In 1900, Lawson attended the WCTU conference in Paris, where she apparently gathered the data for her *Review* article.[23]

Lawson labels alcohol the "dreadful incubus" and "overpowering demon," blasting the government for supporting the sale of intoxicants to generate revenue, echoing Howe's point that the money spent on jails, workhouses, almshouses, and hospitals more than outweighs the benefits (240). Lauding women's efforts through the WCTU, whose membership now tops five hundred thousand worldwide, she also praises the work of numerous organizations, among them the Church of England Temperance Society and the British Woman's Christian Temperance Union, as well as a Scottish writer's several publications on Prohibition (241–42). Lawson also reports on WCTU's recently concluded national convention in Washington, DC, specifically mentioning Harper and another *Review* contributor, Frances Joseph, and noting that delegates had attended a reception hosted by President William McKinley and his wife, Ida, and that WCTU representatives had spoken at forty-five churches, including fifteen Black congregations (242).

Prison Reform and Black Crime

Two contributors, Frances Joseph and Elizabeth McDonald, explicitly linked the problem of intemperance to issues of Black crime and incarceration. Born in Holmesville, Mississippi, on November 25, 1861, Frances Joseph lived with her grandparents until the age of eight but fled with her family to New Orleans after her uncle killed an overseer. She attended school briefly but quit to help support her family after her stepfather's death. Joseph married at age eighteen, bore three children, and subsequently divorced her alcoholic husband. She began her prison reform work in 1894 and in 1906 married Adolph P. Gaudet. She became a recognized figure in both the prison reform and temperance movements, and in 1900 she addressed the Louisiana Conference of the Women's Mite Missionary Society before traveling with Lawson and another woman to the United Kingdom, where she attended the WCTU's world convention and solicited funds to build a home for African American children. By 1902, when the *Times-Democrat* reported that she had been active in prison reform work for nearly ten years and had founded the Industrial Home Association, Joseph had raised one thousand dollars but was seeking an additional four thousand dollars to start construction.[24]

In "Prison Reform Work in New Orleans" (April 1899), Joseph details the episode that led her to her life's calling. The account bears out literary scholar Chanta M. Haywood's argument that Joseph's writings "are religious, but they emphasize religion as a primary factor for racial and social uplift."[25] After meeting a weeping woman whose only son is being sent to the state prison, Joseph returns home and kneels to pray for the mother. God then commands her to visit the prison and pray with the inmates (827–28). There, she meets a murderer preparing to be hanged who has a deathbed conversion experience (829–32). In the ensuing five years, Joseph reports, more than two hundred other inmates experienced conversion, while another eleven hundred "pledged to lead better lives" (832). Joseph's activism also encompassed asking judges to treat African

Americans in the same way that the courts treated whites guilty of the same crimes as well as offering offenders training and education in an industrial home setting. She claims that she and the prison reform association to which she belongs have reduced the number of inmates in New Orleans's prison system from nearly five hundred to ninety (833).

According to Joseph, 803 of the 1,147 inmates in Louisiana's state prison are African American, among them 74 women (833). Joseph reports that when she began her work, judges asked who paid her salary, unwilling to believe that volunteer work occupied the two days of the week when she was not supporting herself as a seamstress (834). Now, however, municipal and court officials as well as the city's newspapers treat her kindly and support her cause (835). Joseph's efforts merited another of Kealing's infrequent editorial notes: she had offered her story only after much "earnest solicitation" and only to encourage other women to take up the cause (850–51).

McDonald, reportedly "the first colored woman to act as a probation officer in the Juvenile Court," performed similar work in Chicago.[26] Born in Virginia in 1862, McDonald married her husband, James, in 1888. The couple appears to have had no children, which may have enabled her to devote much of her adult life to penal reform. McDonald was active in the movement by 1899, when a Chicago newspaper, *The Inter Ocean*, reported that she had attended a meeting at Bethel AME Church to raise funds to send an adult convict's wife home to Tennessee. She was a member of the West Side Woman's Club, which also included Wells-Barnett and Anna Julia Cooper. A deep religious faith appears to have led McDonald, like Joseph, to reform work: her influence reportedly moved three convicted murderers to convert and be baptized into the Hyde Park AME Church. Between 1903 and 1907, *The Broad Ax*, a Black weekly published in Chicago and for a time in Salt Lake City, occasionally ran a column covering McDonald's juvenile reform work and featuring her photograph, with additional coverage continuing for many more years.[27]

FIGURE 4.6. ELIZABETH MCDONALD.
COURTESY NEWSPAPERS.COM.

In 1907 Elizabeth and James McDonald founded the Louise Juvenile Home for Dependent Boys, which was located in their home at 6130 Ada Street in Chicago. They funded the home through her work as a day laborer and his job as a painter at the Union Stock Yards, caring for "hundreds" of women and children "of all nationalities" in the ensuing ten years and renting the cottage next door to meet the overwhelming need. In 1916, they converted the home into the Louise Training School for Colored Boys, and the following year the school moved to a thirty-acre site south of the city. With Elizabeth McDonald in increasingly poor health, however, the school closed in 1920.[28]

McDonald opens "Official Service as a Probation Officer in the Cook County Juvenile Court" (January 1904), with the earlier incident of a young boy paroled into her care whose mother was Irish and whose father was African American. The boy's parents had "wandered from their own church" and had taken to drink (218). McDonald reports that she persuaded them to return to church, taking the boy and his three siblings with them to attend. The family dynamic improved, and she adds that the boy "Eddie," now eighteen years old, helps support the family and care for his younger siblings (218). Other anecdotes concern not only her work with juveniles but also of her work with older prison inmates, among them a German domestic worker who is a reformed thief and a woman who spent fourteen years as a prostitute but is now reformed and married. Like other authors, McDonald relates her work with convicted murders who convert and die at peace, feeling forgiveness for their sins (219–21).

McDonald then moves on to a "more general view" of her work: thirty-six convicts converted; fifty-six cottage meetings to educate and uplift needy members of her community; 350 items of clothing distributed to inmates thanks to her supporters; and 155 visits to the county jail as well others to the penitentiary, police station, and hospitals. She also provides a financial report and thanks Ransom, at the time the pastor of the Institutional Church, and other religious and civic organizations, particularly the Woman's Club of Chicago, for funding and support for her work (225). Kealing urged readers to mail financial contributions to McDonald (225).

Finally, Ida Joyce Jackson addresses the sociological problems of intemperance and Black crime in "Do Negroes Constitute a Race of Criminals?" (April 1907). Ida Joyce was born in Columbus, Ohio, in 1863 and graduated from high school there in 1882. She taught in the public schools of Frankfurt, Kentucky, from 1885 to 1888, then joined the staff of what would become the Kentucky Normal and Industrial Institute for Colored Persons, where she was named an instructor in domestic economy in 1890, a year after marrying the school's president, John Henry Jackson. After he became president of the Lincoln Institute in Jefferson City, Missouri, she studied sociology there (1899–1900). In August 1903 she delivered a paper, "Purity of the Home," at a meeting of the Western Negro Press Association, and the following summer, she represented Colorado at the meeting of the National Association of Colored Women held in St. Louis.[29]

Figure 4.7. Ida Joyce Jackson. Courtesy of HathiTrust Digital Library.

Jackson's thirteen-page article was the text of a speech delivered at Denver's Payne Chapel AME Church that, according to *The Topeka Plaindealer*, had been published previously in *The Denver Daily News*.[30] Reflecting her training in empirical sociology, she states that her "purpose" is "to show by facts, figures and arguments" that African Americans are not inherently criminals (305). Instead, she contends, under slavery, "the dominant race" gave no attention to the ethical education of their human property as well as despoiled African American women. Since emancipation, however, race men and women have sought to protect women's sanctity, and when African Americans have copied the vices of their former enslavers by stealing, they did so only to feed their families (306–7). Jackson asserts that the "best people of the colored race" hold no sympathy with "the criminal element" but insists that Black offenders should not be subject to harsher penalties than whites convicted of the same crimes (308). She attributes the statistic that 85 percent of those incarcerated in the South are African Americans to the fact that whites preside over the courts (308).

Jackson then shifts to statistics about African American accomplishments since the close of the Civil War: illiteracy has been reduced by 45 percent; 2.5 million children are enrolled in public schools; Black writers have published five hundred books; twenty-two thousand African American churches have been built; and African Americans have accumulated farms and houses worth $5 billion. She also tallies the number of high schools, colleges, academies, law schools, medical schools, and seminaries and declares Atlanta the "intellectual mecca" for the race (302–11). She then boldly chides President Theodore Roosevelt for publicly calling Black criminals the "worst enemy" of their race while saying nothing about white criminality, especially lynchings and other attacks on African Americans (311–12). Despite Roosevelt's demand that African Americans "police" their own, few African Americans are employed as policemen, and the "bitter hatred toward the Negro" expressed by Ben Tillman, Thomas Dixon Jr., and other white demagogues goes largely unchecked (313–14). However, she also acknowledges white leaders who have condemned lynch mobs and urged the government to uphold African American rights (316). She concludes that "sociology fails to establish" the criminality of the Black race and looks forward hopefully to a time when "equal rights and opportunities" will be guaranteed to all citizens, "regardless of race or color" (317).

Women contributors to the *A.M.E. Church Review* concerned themselves with social reform and sociological issues from the family, home, and church to broader social issues. As women actively engaged in reform movements across the nation, these women insisted on the centrality of women to the betterment not only of the race but of the larger culture, thus forwarding claims for the rights, duties, and responsibilities of women outside the home. Whether advocating for temperance, suffrage, economic opportunity, or reforms to the criminal justice system, these women left their mark on a host of social institutions during the Progressive Era.

CHAPTER 5

E. Marie Carter's "Notes of Travel" Column, 1903–1912

In January 1902, *Review* editor Hightower T. Kealing published "A Public Acknowledgment and a Plea" (268) in which he praised E. Marie Carter as "the most efficient helper" among the agents soliciting subscriptions for the quarterly. Seeking to find "more like her," he offered to pay women subscription agents between five and ten dollars per week if they could bring in as many new subscriptions as Carter did: "We have repeatedly contended that our girls and women should strike out along new and independent lines of endeavor, and not wait for somebody to give them a salaried job or teaching or housework." The editor added, "Why don't they see their opportunity to make money and travel and be self-supporting all at the same time?" Kealing's solicitation appears quite extraordinary, not only because Jim Crow laws rendered rail travel challenging for African Americans but also because many male contributors took conservative, patriarchal positions regarding women's roles. It appears that few other women stepped forward to become traveling *Review* agents, but Carter spent ten years traveling on behalf of the quarterly, contributing a long-running and evidently quite popular "Notes of Travel" column.

The 2018 film *Green Book* and Candacy Taylor's monumental 2020 work, *The Overground Railroad: The Green Book and the Roots of Black Travel in America*, have brought mainstream attention to the history of Black travel in the United States.[1] However, the excellent scholarship on the subject by Cheryl J. Fish, Carla L. Peterson, and others focuses primarily on book-length works such as the *Narrative of the Travels of Nancy Prince* and the *Autobiography of Amanda Berry Smith*; scholarship on Black travel writing published in periodicals remains sparse.[2] This chapter recovers for a wider audience Carter's largely neglected "Notes of Travel" column. In the only scholarly reference to Carter's column, David W. Wills incorrectly states that it began in 1904, though it first appeared in April 1903, and he then goes on to dismiss her work as "mostly... accounts of churches she visited and spoke in while" traveling for the *Review*: her columns "afford some useful material on A.M.E. history, but little that is important concerning the role of women."[3]

Wills's claim misses the significance of Carter's columns to Black women's intellectual history and periodical studies. Carter's column served as one precursor to the *Green-Book*, demonstrated a generic hybridity, and functioned as a form of feminized sociological writing contributing to a rhetoric of racial uplift.[4] As the work of the Colored Conventions Project and subsequent publications make clear, Black travelers in the nineteenth century would have consulted local advertisements for food and lodging when attending conventions.[5] And as Taylor notes, Victor H. Green modeled *The Negro-Motorist Green-Book*, first published in 1936, on guidebooks for Jewish travelers published earlier in the decade.[6] But long before the emergence of guidebooks, Black travelers would have had to rely on word-of-mouth, address directories (where available), or the Black press, and Carter's columns provided one source of useful information, containing elements of travel writing, history, geography, sociology, and homiletic.

Both Carter and Green sought to render Black travel easier and safer by publishing the names and addresses of locations where readers might find respite. However, both authors tailored their writings to the eras in which they lived and to their audiences. Carter's columns circulated at a time when Black travelers in the South frequently moved via horse-drawn conveyances, and she accordingly mentions stables and liveries. But by the time the *Green-Book* appeared, African Americans had more mobility and prosperity, and the guidebook presumes automobile travel, offering information about taxicabs, service stations, and garages. Carter's column clearly targets an audience comprised primarily of AME Church members and other religiously inclined readers, focusing largely but not exclusively on Black churches and educational institutions and on readers traveling for family or business purposes. Green's book, conversely, includes entries on liquor stores, taverns, nightclubs, barbershops, and beauty parlors but makes no mention of Black churches or educational institutions. Both authors highlight other businesses owned by or welcoming to Black travelers: Carter identifies Black-owned grocery and dry goods stores and confectionaries, all of which flourished in the first decade of the twentieth century, while Green lists hotels, tourist homes, and restaurants that welcomed Black motorists in later years.

Travel for America's Black citizens proved especially challenging during the years when Carter worked for the *Review*. As Miriam Taggert points out, Northern laws and customs regulating segregation on trains and streetcars began in the 1840s and 1850s as formerly enslaved people migrated out of the South. These laws were then "reimagined and revived in the postbellum South," with the "American train compartment" becoming "deeply contested precisely because it served as a mobile repository of a larger culture's racial, gender, and class practices and tensions." Frances Ellen Watkins Harper used her work in the 1860s to decry violence against African Americans related to train and streetcar travel, while Taggert focuses on Anna Julia Cooper, Ida B. Wells-Barnett, and Mary Church Terrell, who complained of their treatment while riding trains in the late nineteenth and early twentieth centuries.[7] African Americans also protested their treatment by boycotting streetcars in more than two dozen cities. Between 1902 and 1912, Carter's travels took her to twenty-two cities holding streetcar boycotts, so she was likely very aware of these protests, but her columns featured only sunny descriptions of her encounters.[8]

Carter's travels predate Booker T. Washington's sojourn in the western United States and its territories, and her accounts of travel through Georgia present a noted contrast to W. E. B. Du Bois's time in Dougherty County, Georgia, as recorded in *The Souls of Black Folk* (1903).[9] While Washington has been credited with encouraging Black settlements in the West, Carter had published accounts of visits to successful Black towns in the Oklahoma and Indian Territories a full four years earlier.[10] Carter's columns provided a female-centric, sociological portrait of the places she travelled, and by doing so, subtly challenged the gender ideology of male AME church members in this era while furthering a feminist-infused rhetoric of racial uplift.

That said, Carter was not the first African American to contribute what can be identified as travel writing to a Black periodical. In 1844, Molliston M. Clark served as a traveling agent for the AME Church, soliciting subscriptions to its publications and selling pamphlets and books, and published in the *African Methodist Episcopal Church Magazine* "a series of essays on life among black people, based on information gleaned during his travel." His success in those endeavors prompted the General Convention to elevate him to the editorship of the denomination's weekly newspaper, *The Christian Recorder*, in 1852, and he later served as executive editor of the denomination's original quarterly, *The Repository of Religion and Literature and of Science and Art*.[11] Moreover, as Eric Gardner has demonstrated, Lizzie Hart also published a series of letters in the *Recorder* in 1864 and 1865 that included tourist-like descriptions of the places she visited.[12] As Mia Bay has shown, Wells published brief accounts of a 1886 train trip through Kansas and Colorado to California in a Baptist periodical, *The Living Way*.[13] And between 1891 and 1895, Levi J. Coppin published an occasional column in the

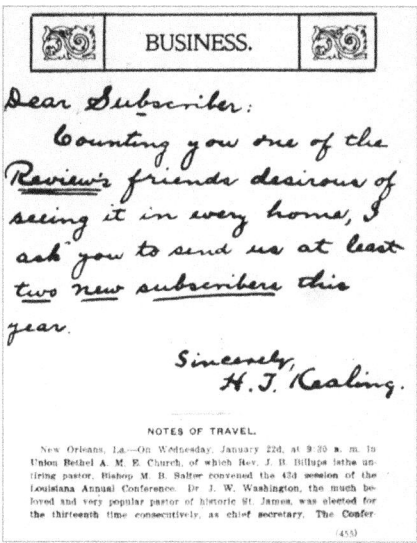

FIGURE 5.1. KEALING'S APPEAL, *A.M.E. CHURCH REVIEW*, APRIL 1909, 455. COURTESY OF SPECIAL COLLECTIONS & ARCHIVES, DREW UNIVERSITY LIBRARIES.

Review, "From the Field," in which he commented on his travel and on which Carter may have modeled her initial columns.

However, none of these fragmented travel writings match the length and detail of Carter's columns, which appeared in more than twenty issues between April 1903 and April 1912, totaled more than 160 pages of writing, and detailed visits to more than 350 different towns and cities. Her columns proved so popular that in the April 1909 "Twenty-fifth Anniversary Issue" of the quarterly, Kealing prefaced the column with a handwritten appeal for each reader to secure two new subscribers.

Between 1903 and 1905, Carter's column appeared annually in the April issue and covered Carter's travel for the previous year. In 1906 and 1907, columns appeared in April and July, with each one covering six months of travel in the previous year. Between January 1910 and April 1912, Carter's columns appeared in every issue. Early columns generally ran between seven and ten pages, but the April 1905 column occupied twenty pages—nearly one-fifth of the issue's total reading matter. Carter included historical information; demographic data; sociological observations; geographic descriptions of cities, rivers, ports, and sites of interest; descriptions of the architecture of AME churches; descriptions of homes and people; and conference proceedings.

Carter was fairly well-known in her day in Black religious and literary circles. Born in New Orleans in 1877, she was of mixed ancestry and described herself as "a Creole by birth, and a little superstitious (all Creoles are)" (April 1904, 382). Her grandmother was of Native American descent, and her grandfather was the brother of Union general Philip Sheridan. Her uncle, Moses Sheridan, the son of a white enslaver and a woman he enslaved, became a prosperous farmer in Greensburg, Louisiana, who donated some of his three hundred thousand acres of land to the AME denomination, which named the Sheridan AME Chapel in his honor. Carter attended New Orleans University and launched her first lecture tour in 1896, speaking in the North and East on behalf of southern black women. In 1900, Carter spoke at Wilberforce University's commencement services and was described as having "traveled very extensively." Three years later, she was appointed as an "evangelist" to the Quincy District of the AME Church. By 1911, she was "regarded as one of the ablest women in the denomination to which she belongs."[14]

Carter apparently met her future husband, the Reverend Charles Wesley Newton, during an August 1909 stopover in Joplin, Missouri. He evidently made quite an impression, prompting her not only to describe him as "the very successful and popular pastor of Handy A.M.E. Church" but to note, "It's positively known that whoever is the guest of Dr. Newton enjoys a royal entertainment. He is truly a prince in making sunshine for all who pass his way" (July 1910, 104). It is unclear when the two married, and little is known of her life after 1912, but Newton's ministry eventually took them to St. Louis, where they died under mysterious circumstances in 1927.[15]

The above is the likeness of Miss E. Marie Carter of New Orleans, La., who started ont on a lecturing tour in 1896. The first daughter of the south, she has traveled very extensively in the north and east speaking for "The Black Women of the South." She is spoken of in glowing terms as the "Princess of Oratory." She has done some very excellent Missionary work for the parent Mite Missionary Society, and in 1899 organized some 33 societies of Home and Foreign Missions under the direction of Bishop A. Grant. She is added to our staff of associates and listen to hear from her pen.

* * *

FIGURE 5.2. E. MARIE CARTER, FROM *MISSIONARY SEARCHLIGHT*, JANUARY 15, 1900. COURTESY NEWSPAPERS.COM.

As an agent of the *Review*, Carter's job consisted of traveling to various AME district conferences to both solicit subscriptions for the quarterly and sell books published by the AME Book Concern. On March 5, 1902, in Jacksonville, Florida, she "sold all books sent from the Review Department" (April 1903, 775). Similarly, in Live Oak, Florida, on February 16, 1903, "many books were sold and a large subscription secured for THE REVIEW" (April 1904, 380). She was also addressing meetings of the Allen Christian Endeavor League by 1905 (April 1906, 388) and was serving as its field secretary at the time of its February 24, 1909, session of the South Florida Conference held in Palatka (January 1910, 311).[16]

Carter traveled for nearly the entire year, taking only a week or two of rest around the Christmas and Easter holidays. She frequently traveled alone, though she occasionally accompanied AME bishops and other church officials. District conferences appear to have been scheduled to accommodate the climate, with Southern conventions generally held in the winter and spring and Northern conventions generally occurring during the summer and fall. Carter usually traveled by rail and steamship on longer journeys but preferred to go via electric car or via horse-drawn conveyances on shorter trips. On one occasion, she rode six miles in an oxcart to visit her uncle, Moses Sheridan, after he did not learn of her impending visit in time to meet her via electric car: "I can assure my kind readers there is some difference in the travel of an ox-cart and an electric car" (April 1906, 389).

Such quips were generally the closest Carter came to complaining about travel conditions. The sole exception was her report from Croom, Florida, that "as usual little or no attention is given to the waiting room for the Colored people in these villages. Not a heater at Croom, not even a light. Mr. Williams and Rev. Berrian had to furnish a lamp, and on this cold morning, Friday, Feb. 28, made a bon fire, and before the fire the representative of the *Review* waited for the train" (April 1909, 458). In contrast, her contemporaries Cooper and Wells railed against the indignities of traveling while a Black female.[17] Such indignities ran counter to the etiquette of train travel, under which women were expected to demonstrate genteel behavior and could expect appropriate treatment in return.[18] If Carter was subject to harsh treatment, she declined to present that information to the readers of the *Review*. Whether a mark of her Christian forbearance, an accommodationist attitude, or a deliberate strategy of silence on the matter of unequal travel conditions for white and Black passengers, Carter's breezy descriptions of pleasant stays and warm receptions likely glossed over the hardships inherent in her work on behalf of the AME Church.

Carter instead focused on identifying segments of rail lines, noting connections, stops, and terminus points. For example, she notes one trip that took her "three hundred and sixty-six miles from Jacksonville to Miami, the terminus of the Florida East Coast Railroad and its several steamboat connections" (April 1904, 380). Between Jupiter and West Palm Beach, the train passed the "Hotel

Royal Poinciana, the Breakers and scores of handsome cottages," gushing that "the writer feels that the most expressive adjective in her vocabulary is too insignificant to even suggest her delight at the matchless and majestic view that greeted her eyes before she left the train" (, 380).[19] While traveling in Mississippi the following year, she notes, "Jackson, with a population of 7,816 is fast becoming one of the greatest railroad centers in the South" (April 1905, 375).

Carter also comments on the people she encounters. While journeying from Greenville, Mississippi, to the Central Florida Conference at Ocala, she found that the conductors, most of whom were white men, "are very obliging; they run their train slow enough for one to transact any business along the line" (April 1904, 386).[20] Her business would presumably have included posting and collecting letters, arranging for packages, and resting and dining with local families. On her way to the South Florida Conference in February 1909, "Mr. A. E. Ladner, the Division Passenger Agent of the L. and N. Railway granted me a stop-over in Mobile on Sunday February 21 which was spent pleasantly and profitably in the service of the Lord" (310). And en route from High Springs, Florida, to the "beautiful village" of Plains, Georgia, in March 1910, "I had two very pleasant and profitable stop overs, waiting for the train, first at Lake City, Florida . . . second at Cordele, Georgia." In both cities she was met and entertained by local residents who "were really glad that I missed my train . . . and delighted to have me stop over" (January 1911, 315). While aboard the steamer *Hessie* from Brunswick to Darien, Georgia, she found "first class accommodations for first class fare" (January 1910, 311).

Arrangements for Carter's accommodations appear generally to have been made before she arrived in town, and her hosts would meet her at the train and swiftly conduct her to their homes. After visiting her aunt in Hannibal, Missouri, Carter arrived in Chicago at 2:30 p.m., and "in a few minutes my stopping place was passed to me. At a glance I saw that I was to be the guest of Dr. and Mrs. D. P. Roberts and their four little daughters" (October 1908, 128). Carter continues, "I shall never forget the warm welcome given me by dear Mrs. Roberts, who knows fully how to make one feel truly at home." "To know her is to love her," Carter declares, using a phrase she often repeated.[21]

The detailed descriptions Carter provided of her hosts—full names, occupations, and often street addresses—announced a network of caring individuals (some of whom were not AME members) likely to come to the aid of other Black travelers. In Leesburg, Florida, for example, she was welcomed into the "comfortable home" of the Reverend W. J. Sanders, a leading minister in the AME Zion denomination, and his wife (January 1911, 311).

Carter's accounts mention only three commercial lodgings: the Florida hotel mentioned previously, the Mount Vernon Hotel in Norfolk, Virginia, and the YWCA of Brooklyn, New York, of which, she was a member. The Mount Vernon Hotel, owned by Lemuel W. Bright, is "first class in every particular; the interior is quite artistic, the rooms are well-furnished, and everything had an aura of fine taste" (April 1909, 464). For its part, the Brooklyn YWCA "offers to colored women the use of attractive, comfortable rooms, where members may find recreation, entertainment, companionship and welcome, enjoying the benefits of religious and educational advantages" (April 1907, 383–84). Carter likely found few commercial establishments willing to accept Black travelers, and paying for accommodations would have counteracted the primary purpose of her constant travel—raising funds for the church. By showcasing hospitable Black homes and prosperous Black businesses, however, Carter constructed a national Black travel network.

"Notes of Travel" on History, Geography, and Sociology

Carter's brief descriptions of the towns and cities she visited offer more detailed historical and geographical information than Green provides. Her April 1904 column includes lengthy descriptions of numerous Florida cities—St. Augustine, Daytona, New Smyrna, West Palm Beach, Titusville, Miami, Orlando, Live Oak, Leesburg—likely because her northern readers knew very little about the "land of flowers," which had underdeveloped rail and road systems.[22] An extended description of Boston and Cambridge, Massachusetts, appears in the "Miscellaneous" section of the October 1906 issue (176–79).

In April 1905, Carter writes about her 1904 sojourn in Indian Territory and Oklahoma Territory. In South MacAlester, Indian Territory, on April 13, 1904, she stayed "at the very comfortable home of Mr. and Mrs. James W. Johnson, one of the leading Negro merchants" (379). Four days later, she visited St. Paul's AME Church in Guthrie, Oklahoma Territory, a "beautiful town" with "a population of 10,006" that she declares "is the equal of and really surpasses many cities in the States" (379). In summarizing her visit to the territories, she offers the same level of detailed sociological observations that Washington provides four years later:

> I am pleased to state that I found in all cities visited in the territories, Negroes in the commercial world. At South McAlester, Mr. J. W. Johnson has a first-class grocery store and ice cream parlor. At Wewoka, several young men have a joint grocery store on the main street in the town. At Wagoner Mr. C. H. Smith is the proprietor of general merchandise and owns the large brick building, which is full of excellent stock. At Okmulgee Mr. J. B. Key, dealer in general merchandise, corner of Fourth and Morton Avenue, owns stores in Okmulgee I.T. and Luther O.T. I had the pleasure of beholding the very fine stone front building at Okmulgee I.T., containing a full supply of fresh first-class goods. Mr. Key stated to me "that the territory needs monied men, men of brains and grit; that now is the time to come purchase land and open business." A man with an eye to business can reap for himself a golden harvest. (381)

But scholars overlooked Carter's sociological observations, like those of many of her African American sisters, instead crediting the later work of male writers. Carter's "Notes of Travel" definitely concern themselves with sociological issues such as racial demographics, occupations, landownership, accumulated wealth, creation of cultural institutions, religion, and reform work.

Carter works to entertain and orient her readers, at times injecting humor into her writing. She offers a rhyming description of Poplar Bluff, Missouri, as a "hilly town, where you are first up and then down" (April 1905, 387) and labels Little Rock, Arkansas, the "city of 'Small Stones'" (April 1904, 385). While in Gainesville, Florida, in February–March 1905, she visits the nearby "Alachua sink," a "strange body of water, which has no visible outlet, and is supposed to be relieved through subterranean channels to the Gulf or Atlantic" (April 1906, 390). To give readers a frame of reference, she compares Southern locales to Northern cities: Chattanooga is the "Pittsburg of Tennessee" (July 1906, 91), while Natchez, Mississippi, is the "Boston of the South" (January 1910, 309).

Carter's columns take on a more sociological bent beginning in 1905, constituting a form of feminized sociology. Carter would undoubtedly have read the *Review*'s "Sociological" column, and she likely had read Du Bois's published work in the *Review* and in *The Souls of Black Folk*.[23] In that 1903 volume, Du Bois reports on his tour through Dougherty County in southwestern Georgia—via train through Macon and Albany and by car from there. Du Bois focuses on the "nine million men" who make their home in the state: his vignettes primarily involve male subjects, and the people whose names he provides are Joe Fields, Harrison Gohagen, Dark Carter, Luke Black, and Pa Willis.[24] Carter, in contrast, notes the achievements of Black men and women, demonstrating "that truly the Negro is rising" (July 1908, 84). Between 1902 and 1909, Carter visited more than two dozen towns and cities from Columbus, on Georgia's western border with Alabama, across to Darien on the east coast, and down to St. Marys, just above the border with Florida to the south. Carter's observations seem to be designed particularly to challenge the bleak picture of rural Georgia painted by Du Bois.[25]

Unlike the "straggling, unlovely villages" he describes, Carter sees thriving small communities.[26] For example, in the "very enterprising town of Ocilla," population seven thousand, African Americans "own beautiful homes" (April 1907, 381). The major businesses in Fitzgerald include "large grocery stores, meat markets, men's clothing stores, and drugstore" (381). Also pronounced "very enterprising" is Valdosta, population twelve thousand, with "two schools and sixteen churches" serving the fifty-five hundred "quite progressive" African Americans living there (July 1908, 83–84). Carter praises the "quaint town" of Darien for the inhabitants' "race pride" and reform work, demonstrated in the establishment of the Saint Cyprian Mission and the Industrial School (January 1910, 311). Carter focuses on achievements rather than tribulations, presenting a feminized view of racial uplift through enterprise, homeownership, education, and reform work.

Carter also marshals demographic data in her accounts. Bonita, Louisiana, was "thickly settled by Negroes, more than one-third of whom own their homes"; forty-one miles away, Monroe has a population of 6,428, with "eight churches for colored people" (April 1905, 375, 376). Mound Bayou, Mississippi, constitutes "a quite enterprising town, the entire population Negroes" (390). Langhorne, Pennsylvania, is a "beautiful borough, twenty-two miles from Philadelphia, with a population of 800, two hundred of which are colored people" (July 1906, 86). The four thousand residents of Union Springs, Alabama, include sixteen hundred African Americans (June 1906, 93). And among the eight hundred people in Hollandale, Mississippi, "60% are Negroes who own comfortable homes" (October 1911, 624). Turning her attention to her home city, she observes that New Orleans is the country's twelfth-largest city and that its population of three hundred thousand (more than half as many as Boston) is about one-quarter African American (April 1907, 379). The five thousand residents of the "mining town" of Boxton, Iowa, include four thousand African Americans (July 1907, 83). And in Lakeland, Florida, among "a population of 3,012, 1000 are Negroes" (July 1908, 83).

FIGURE 5.3. MOUND BAYOU, MISS. COURTESY THE LIBRARY COMPANY OF PHILADELPHIA READING ROOM.

RHETORICS OF RACIAL UPLIFT: BLACK-OWNED BUSINESSES AND EDUCATIONAL INSTITUTIONS

Carter's rhetoric of racial uplift reflects the views of Washington and Wells. As was the case for Du Bois, Carter likely had read Washington's contributions to the *Review* as well as *Character Building*, a 1903 collection of his addresses to the students at Tuskegee Institute.[27] Washington stresses homeownership in a number of these addresses, particularly "On Getting a Home," and Wells does the same in her essay "The Requisites of True Leadership" (1891), in which she embraces "Progress" in terms of "Education, Character, Wealth, and Unity" and urges the Black man to save his money to "educate himself and his children, buy a home, and go into business."[28] Echoing Washington and Wells, Carter describes a September 1904 trip to Cairo, Illinois, where "many of our people own beautiful homes, which are elegantly furnished" (April 1905, 387). Carter links homeownership to progress in her description of her March 1904 visit to Texarkana, Texas: "The colored population of this town is striving to be progressive. A large number own beautiful homes" (376). Like Washington, Carter emphasizes not only homeownership, but ownership of land as well. She observes that the "colored people" in Harrodsburg, Kentucky, "own valuable land and comfortable homes" (July 1906, 90). Popular, Louisiana, "is really a Negro settlement, a large percentage owning their own homes and farms" (April 1905, 375).

Many of Carter's entries note not only ownership of property but also business endeavors. For example, following a visit to the Hunter Institute in Jones, Louisiana, she reports that the proprietor "owns one thousand acres of land" and earned eight thousand dollars from cotton sales in 1903 (April 1905, 376). In Arcadia, Florida, five families together own a grocery store, a confectionary, and a soda fountain, while another citizen had owned nothing a few years earlier but now possesses twenty-seven city lots, thereby proving that "the Negro is capable of being at the head of his own enterprise" (July 1908, 82).

Later descriptions of homes and other edifices stress their up-to-date conveniences. Visiting the Reverend G. W. Allen, editor of *The Southern Christian Recorder*, and his wife, Phoebe Harvey Allen, in Columbus, Georgia, in March 1909, she was delighted to find an excellent dinner in the Allens' "modern, beautiful, and comfortable home" (April 1910, 410).[29] Three months later, Carter was the guest of Mr. and Mrs. Percy Miller of Catskill, New York, where they lived in a "beautiful home with all modern improvements" that was "centrally located" at 175 Main Street (415).

Carter also lauds the "modern improvements" she encountered during a November 1909 visit to her "very dear friends," Bishop Elias Cottrell and Catherine Cottrell, in Holly Springs, Mississippi, where he had founded Mississippi Industrial College in 1906. The newest building, Catherine Hall, named for the founder's wife, was "made of pressed brick ... rooms lighted by electricity [and] heated by steam" (October 1910, 206).

Carter's reportage regarding Mississippi Industrial College reflects her prioritization of visits to educational and other institutions created by and/or for African Americans. Her columns record more than thirty stops at normal institutes, colleges, universities, industrial homes, hospitals, and sanitariums. Whereas early writings focused on institutes for agricultural and industrial education, later

FIGURE 5.4. CATHERINE HALL, MISSISSIPPI INDUSTRIAL COLLEGE. COURTESY THE LIBRARY COMPANY OF PHILADELPHIA READING ROOM.

entries highlight the benefits of both industrial education and classical courses of instruction, perhaps reflecting the ongoing debates between Washington and Du Bois over the type and purpose of higher education for African Americans or perhaps indicating the growing influence of Du Bois's view that African Americans should not limit themselves to agricultural and manual education but should pursue employment as merchants, captains of industry, physicians, lawyers, advanced teachers, ministers, scientists, and artists.[30]

Carter visited Tuskegee Institute in November 1905, traveling "forty-three miles in a surrey in one day" in her eagerness to get there (July 1906, 92). She met with Washington the following August when she attended the National Negro Business League, receiving "royal treatment" (July 1907, 83). However, she never mentions Du Bois by name.

The July 1906 "Notes on Travel" includes a two-and-a-half-page account of Carter's December 1905 visit to the Alabama State Normal School for Negroes, located in Huntsville. She combines a description of the grounds and architecture (including the president's residence, which had formerly been the home of General Andrew Jackson) with a brief history of the founding of the school, a biography of its president, William Hooper Council, a description of Christmas Day services, and an overview of the curriculum.

In March 1909, Carter visited Ballard Normal School in Macon, Georgia. In her account, she explicitly connects the school's success

FIGURE 5.5. BALLARD NORMAL SCHOOL. COURTESY THE LIBRARY COMPANY OF PHILADELPHIA READING ROOM.

FIGURE 5.6. WESTERN UNIVERSITY. COURTESY THE LIBRARY COMPANY OF PHILADELPHIA READING ROOM.

to the contributions of AME Church members: "This school is entirely without endowment and dependent for its support upon the American Missionary Association and the tuition received from students. The school was established in 1865 by the Freedmen's Bureau. It is the purpose of this institution to offer to the colored people of central Georgia the best possible opportunities for obtaining a standard high school education, with special normal and industrial training. The school has 15 teachers, ten white and five colored Three of the five are loyal members of the A.M.E. Church" (April 1910, 409).

The shift in emphasis from agricultural/mechanical institutions to those that also offer classical courses is evident in Carter's April 1912 column, which records her visit to Kansas's Western University, where Kealing was now serving as president after leaving the editorship of the *A.M.E. Church Review*. Carter's tribute to her mentor of nearly a dozen years, describes the school's commencement exercises, highlighting the College, Academic, Industrial, and Music Department's as well as Carter's address regarding "Our President" (831–33).

Churches and Parsonages

Carter's descriptions of the many churches she visited no doubt provided readers with a rich sense of the steady growth of their faith tradition in all parts of the country. Her initial accounts prove fairly brief: of two 1904 stops in Louisiana, she writes simply, "We have a beautiful church at Patterson" and the Bonita church is "very spacious" (April 1905, 374, 375). But Kealing apparently was interested in depicting physical facilities, adding a feature column on "Architecture in the A.M.E. Church" to the October 1903 issue. Kealing promised "free to every subscriber of the A.M.E. Review" a "great three-color chromotype of the A.M.E. Church in Vicksburg, Mississippi" (October 1903, cover); and including expensive engravings in several later issues (April 1904, April 1905, October 1905).[31] Perhaps because of the costs of such engravings, Kealing may well have encouraged Carter to include brief architectural descriptions in her column whenever possible, thereby satisfying AME members' curiosity about other churches as well as promoting pride in the denomination's rapid growth.

In Florida in March 1907, Carter proclaims, "Fort Myers can truly boast of the prettiest church on the Atlantic coast line." Moreover, the church was planned and built by the Reverend M. D. Potter: "Every nail was driven by his hand. A most magnificent church. . . . Just think of it, not one cent charged for his labor" (July 1908, 82). Potter was also responsible for "another beautiful church," Mt. Zion AME, at her next stop, Arcadia (82).[32]

Carter's descriptions of church interiors subsequently become noticeably more detailed and elaborate and echo her focus on the modernity of residences. In Seabright, New Jersey, she praises the pastor and members of the "up-to-date" St. Luke AME Church, "a brick building, with Georgia pine rafters and Gothic roof." She continues, "The magnificent picture in the front window is 'Jesus and the woman at the well.' The pulpit and chairs are made of the cedar of Lebanon, colonial style. They are exquisite" (October 1908, 126). Attending the June 1909 Ohio state convention of the Allen Christian Endeavor League in Cleveland, she declares St. John's AME Church, built in 1908 at East 40th Street and Central Avenue, "really and truly the finest in the Connection. Modern in every particular, thoroughly completed, the very best of material, a most excellent location." She enthuses, "Too much praise cannot be given to dear" Dr. Ira Collins, "a master builder" and the church's pastor (July 1910, 101).[33]

Such opulence constituted evidence of race prosperity, another theme of Carter's writings. When she arrived in Little Rock, Arkansas, in October 1910, the minister at Bethel AME, J. Oscar Iverson, was in the midst of relocating to a new, larger parsonage and a "magnificent church" was under construction: "When completed, it will be the largest, the finest, and the leading church edifice in the 9th Episcopal District," and "Dr. Iverson and his good people deserve much credit for the splendid work being done" (October 1911, 623).

Carter's final column describes the opulence of Baltimore's Bethel Church, which had been built in 1868 as St. Peter's Protestant Episcopal Church at a cost of $250,000 and purchased by the AME denomination for $90,000 in 1910. Its excellent location on Druid Hill Avenue provides "easy access for hundreds to attend." After declaring that "words fail me to describe the magnificent church building," she resolves to "make the attempt": "The wall back of the pulpit and the base of the pulpit are of fine mosaic inlaid with hundreds of small golden crosses, made in Italy at a cost of several hundred thousand dollars. The pulpit is a beautiful white marble, on either side, seven golden candlesticks. The main auditorium will seat two thousand; the Sunday School room will seat five hundred; the lecture room, five hundred; a total of three thousand can be seated comfortably in beautiful Bethel. The race has many magnificent churches in this city, but Bethel is the largest and most costly of all" (April 1912, 830).[34] The Black denomination's purchase of a church previously housing white worshippers would have been a source of tremendous race pride to Carter's readers.

As in Little Rock, the addition of parsonages in communities throughout the country, indicated the AME Church's increasing wealth and stability. The first mention of a parsonage appears in the April 1905 column, with descriptions becoming increasingly frequent over the next five years. In St. George, South Carolina, the Reverend P. M. Monzon and his "dear people" had built a "spacious two-story parsonage" and undertaken the "remodeling of the church" in 1906 (July 1907, 90). Between January and May 1908, she saw parsonages of note in Dunnelon and Dade City, Florida, and Brunswick, Georgia, as well as a "beautiful church and parsonage" in Cape May, New Jersey (April 1909, 458, 459, 462). The following year, however, Carter mentions no parsonages, probably because they had become nearly ubiquitous even in smaller towns.

Carter's emphasis on church interiors and comfortable parsonages enabled her to stress the importance of the labor and financial support of the AME denomination's women members. The elaborate description of the interior of St. Paul's AME Church, in Malvern, Arkansas, credits the efforts of the church's women's auxiliary, the Busy Bee Club, which "purchased a beautiful pulpit for the church and are now arranging to put in electric lights" (April 1905, 378). On another occasion, she notes that a "beautiful carpet" covering the church rostrum had been purchased by the pastor's wife and "the faithful women of the church" (July 1907, 88)

Advocating for Expanding Roles for Women

In keeping with pious feminism and the conservative views about gender roles espoused by most of the *Review*'s male contributors (and presumably readers), Carter's challenges to the denomination's gender ideologies are necessarily rather muted. Like Katherine Tillman and others, Carter uses the rhetorical strategy of stressing the primacy of women's work inside the home to advocate for expanded roles in the wider world.

From her earliest columns, Carter singles out women's achievements, praising, for example, "Mrs. M. Walker," who is "active in business" as well as in "church work" (April 1905, 384). In 1906, she comments on Sallie Rickett's ownership of a livery and on three women homeowners in Centralia, Illinois (July 1906, 89). Two years later, she notes that in Tampa, Florida, Mattie Lee owns "one of the largest livery, feed and sale stables" and is engaged in the undertaking and embalming business (July 1908, 81).

Carter pays particular homage to the contributions of women to the church, to clubs, and to reform work. She praises the Phillis Wheatley Club and Christian Culture Congress of Buffalo, New York, before whom she delivered an address in June 1905 (April 1906, 394). In Danville, Illinois, the Lively Eight young people's club, Women's Aid Circle, and Sewing Circle combined to provide the chandelier, circle window over the pulpit, and furnace to the church where the Illinois Conference convened in September 1906 (July 1907, 84). Addressing the Women's Progressive Club of Chester, Pennsylvania, on May 24, 1907, she observes that the club's goal is to establish "a day nursery and a working girls' home" (July 1908, 88). She tells readers about her visits to the Emerson Industrial Home outside Ocala, Florida, founded by Mrs. C. M. Buckbee (April 1904, 386–87) and to the Colored Orphan Industrial Home near Lexington, Kentucky, founded in 1892 by E. Belle Jackson (July 1906, 87–88), as well as about the two-hundred-member Empty Stocking and Fresh Air Circle, which raised $430 toward the purchase of a playground for the "poor children of Baltimore" (April 1911, 416).

Carter also notes approvingly the activities of the individual women and groups involved in active AME ministries. In October 1908, Carter reports that Bishop Henry McNeal Turner "has a large number of women traveling as superintendents, deaconesses, first and second lieutenants," and the like (128). Carter takes special notice of the few occasions when AME churchwomen served as platform speakers for the main sessions at denomination conferences. For example, she lauds the four women who delivered "first class" welcoming addresses at the January 1910 session of the Louisiana Conference (January 1911, 311). In another instance, she praises Mary Evans, a "young Evangelist" who "preached to a crowded house" in Cambridge, Maryland (April 1910, 412).

Carter's reportage on Lena Mason also demonstrates her awareness of the controversy surrounding the status of AME women preachers and the licensing of women evangelists. Lena Doolin was born in May 1864 and married George Mason in 1885. Newspaper reports began identifying her as "the Rev. Lena Mason" in 1894, and she apparently was licensed to preach in the AME denomination by the Reverend Cornelius T. Shaffer. A popular speaker on the Negro Chautauqua circuit as well, Mason was described in 1918 as the "world's greatest female evangelist."[35]

Carter first mentions Mason in July 1906, noting that Bishop Sims had requested that she prepare for the West Kentucky Conference at Owensboro and that she had raised more than two hundred dollars in less than two weeks "from the dear people, white and colored" (91). By October 1907, Carter reports, Mason had become "the very popular pastor of Trinity A.M.E. Church" (October 1908, 131). And in the spring of 1909, according to Carter, "of all the evangelists who have visited" Philadelphia, "Rev. Mason" "appeared to have the largest amount of personal magnetism" (April 1909, 462).

By October 1910, Carter's understanding of the status of the popular evangelist had shifted, as is evidenced by the omission of the title *Reverend*. From this point forward, Carter refers to "Mrs. Lena Mason, Evangelist," likely indicating that Carter had been made aware that in the eyes of the male hierarchy, Mason was considered an evangelist but not an ordained minister.[36] Carter nevertheless continues her praise of Mason, noting that in September 1910, she reported an astounding 332 conversions and $8901.68 in money raised (July 1911, 523).

FIGURE 5.7. LENA MASON. FROM THE NEW YORK PUBLIC LIBRARY DIGITAL COLLECTIONS.

PROMOTING RACIAL HARMONY, EXHORTATIONS, AND HOMILETICS

Though the *Review*'s primary audience was members of the AME Church, the publication also targeted a wider audience that included not only Afro-Protestant readers but white supporters as well. Carter frequently references how white citizens in various locales received church representatives. For example, the Reverend P. W. Williams of Bonita, Louisiana, is "much loved, not only by his members, but by members and friends of all the churches in Bonita and vicinity," while the Reverend W. P. Meyers of Barnesville, Ohio, "has the highest esteem of not only the colored people . . . but of the leading white citizens" (April 1905, 375, 382). When Carter arrived in Cambridge, Ohio, in 1904, "the leading white citizens as well as my own race gave me a cordial welcome" (382). When the Oklahoma Conference convened in October 1906, "the white citizens gave liberally to the support of the Conference" (July 1907, 87). In Darien, Georgia, the African American postmaster, marshal, and inspector of customs are "highly respected by white and black" (January 1910, 312), as were Rev. Walters of Binghamton, New York (July 1910, 100), and the Reverend Green Price of Mayfield, Kentucky (July 1911, 520). When Carter spoke to the Women's Progressive Club of Chester, Pennsylvania, she found a "most excellent audience" and "tried to interest my listeners on 'A White Life for Both'" (July 1908, 88), presumably urging her white audience to support equal opportunities for members of both races. In short, Carter seeks to persuade readers that her travels and other AME conferences and activities promoted racial harmony.

Carter was not a preacher, identifying herself only as "a Representative of the *Review*" (July 1908, 82) and the "Field Secretary" of the Allen Christian Endeavor League (January 1910, 311), and characterizing her stage appearances as "lectures" or "addresses." In April 1903, Carter delivered "an Easter address" at St. Philip Monumental AME Church, in Savannah, Georgia, at which "all persons were very anxious to see the very important picture My Soul and I," an engraving of which had been published in the April 1903 *Review* to illustrate the poem by Robert E. Ford appearing on pages 751–52 (April 1904, 381).[37]

Most of Carter's early addresses were specifically designed to solicit subscriptions for the *Review* and to promote other Black publications and events. For example, an address before the Amityville, New York, Sunday school convention focused on the objectives of the series *Twelve Minor Prophets* (April 1905, 384). At a meeting of the Hagerstown District Conference held in Frederick, Maryland, in the summer of 1905, Carter read a report on the recent meeting of the National Business League (July 1906, 87). At an October 14, 1906, joint meeting of the Baptist Young People's Union and the Allen Christian Endeavor League in Kansas City, Missouri, Carter spoke on "the work of the League and a historical sketch of the same" (July 1907, 85–86). In Langhorne, Pennsylvania, on June 2, 1907, she gave the address at a Children's Day service on "The Possibility of the Young" (July 1908, 89). On March 24, 1908, Carter addressed "the public" regarding "Progress, Reform, and Evolution" (April 1909, 460), a topic to which she returned when she spoke to a chapter of the Allen Christian Endeavor League in Springfield, Missouri, on March 27, 1910 (January 1911, 316). After her April 5, 1909, speech at the Soldiers Home in Kansas City, listeners received copies of "The Marked Characteristics of the Negro Race," an address given by West Virginia governor Albert Blakeslee White.[38] Speaking on July 9, 1909, to the twenty thousand attendees at the World's United Christian Endeavor conference, Carter delivered "Personal Work, the Demand of the Hour" (July 1910, 102), a speech she recycled for the May 1911 commencement ceremony at Western University (April 1912, 832). At Bethel AME Church, in Little Rock, Arkansas, on October 23, 1910, Carter spoke on "The Young People's Movement" (October 1911, 623), while "A Missionary Journal Around the World" was the topic of her January 29, 1911, address to the Allen Christian Endeavor League in Baton Rouge, Louisiana (January 1912, 727).

Carter occasionally lapses into homiletic prose, designed to admonish or exhort. Speaking of an April 1904 trip to Wagoner, Indian Territory, she notes that she has "never visited any city without leaving the Review, which is my sole object. What we most need to do is to put good literature in the homes of our people" (April 1905, 380). Of the "millionaires" who summer in Greenwich, Connecticut, she observes, "They have the means, and now if we could only get them to have the disposition to relieve some of our institutions of learning, a great burden would be removed from many anxious hearts" (383). Carter opines that while the women traveling in Bishop Turner's entourage are "collecting moneys for Africa, I would advise that they tarry awhile and teach these dear people in the rural districts in Georgia how to live in this the Twentieth Century": "I truly believe that the greatest need for missionaries is at home. We need women who are truly consecrated to the work, who will have heart to heart talks with the girls, the young women, and the mothers. No race can rise above the level of its women" (October 1908, 128, 127). Similarly, she hopes that ministers will teach "the people, and especially the young that the offering is of a necessity and that it is a part of the service" (October 1911, 624).

Carter's role as a platform speaker at both religious and lay events brought her in contact with leading Black intellectuals and prominent figures not only in the AME denomination but in other Afro-Protestant religious and social movements. In that respect, "Notes of Travel" often resembles the social columns found in both white and Black nonsectarian periodicals of the day. She rubbed elbows with Booker T. Washington; was entertained by Fanny Jackson Coppin; traveled with or shared the podium with Bishops Levi J. Coppin, Benjamin T. Tanner, Henry McNeal Turner, Benjamin W. Arnett, Grant, Shaffer, Lee, and Derrick, among others. Yet despite her prominence, Carter's labors garnered little recognition. After Reverdy C. Ransom assumed editorship of the *Review* in 1912, Carter disappears from its pages, and she is entirely absent from R. R. Wright's *Encyclopaedia of the African Methodist Episcopal Church* (1947).

In April 1913, "Echoes from the 12th Episcopal District," a column authored by Nora F. Taylor, announced to readers that Ransom had given Taylor "the exalted position of Representative of the *A.M.E. Review*" (412). Taylor's column appeared on only one other occasion (July 1914), and she subsequently spent years as a missionary in Africa. Nonetheless, she received an obituary in the October 1923 *Review*, which also included her photo as the frontispiece, captioned, "The late Nora F. Taylor, Missionary Evangelist Saint." Yet Carter's decade-plus of service to the quarterly and the AME Church merited no such acknowledgment. She simply disappeared from her denomination's historical record.

If Harriet Tubman is considered a key figure in the Underground Railroad, with its nodes of refuge, hospitality, and information exchange, then E. Marie Carter played an analogous part in constructing a capacious, open, and aboveground African American community network during the Progressive Era. Carter's "Notes of Travel" offer her readers a strategy for avoiding some of the indignities of Jim Crow travel by seeking out flourishing Afro-Protestant business, social, and cultural institutions. Anticipating *The Negro Motorist Green-Book*, Carter's columns served as a beacon for Black travelers, as a form of feminized sociology, as an inspiration for racial uplift, and as a celebration of the achievements of AME womanhood.

CHAPTER 6

Matters Educational

As Adam Fairclough notes in *A Class of Their Own: Black Teachers in the Segregated South*, "The confusing nomenclature of black schools—institute, academy, college, university, seminary, training school, normal school, industrial school, normal and industrial school—reflected something of their diversity. But they sometimes offered few clues as to their individual character."[1] In addition to these facilities, local Black communities operated numerous "Sabbath schools," "Sunday schools," and "select schools."[2] However, the fact that so many institutions were created—regardless of their specific nomenclature—demonstrates the importance that Black communities ascribed to education during the Progressive Era. Like home- and landownership, education was seen as essential to racial uplift. That importance is also reflected in the number of articles on the subject that appeared in the *A.M.E. Church Review*—nearly one hundred between 1884 and 1924. But only ten of those essays came from female contributors.[3] Four of those seven contributors—Belle Dorce, Hannah Jones, Nellie Freeman, and Mattie F. Roberts—have previously received little or no notice from scholars of Black education.

Recent scholarship has amply demonstrated the centrality of Black women in promoting racial uplift through education. As Elizabeth McHenry points out, a strong connection existed between the establishment of Black literary societies and the push for widespread literacy.[4] Heather Andrea Williams traces free and enslaved African Americans' efforts to secure literacy before and during the Civil War, including local Black communities' roles in building and supporting American Missionary Association schools, which "could just as easily have been called freedpeople's schools."[5] Gholdy Muhammad cites McHenry's work to argue that literary societies can serve as the model for twenty-first-century "historically responsive literacy."[6] Karen A. Johnson, Abul Pitre, and Kenneth L. Johnson provide extended biobibliographic essays on a host of little-known Black women educators in both the North and the South, while Audrey Thomas McCluskey focuses specifically on Lucy Craft Laney, Mary McLeod Bethune, Charlotte Hawkins Brown, and Nannie Helen Burroughs, four Southern Black women educators who were close friends.[7] And Crystal Lynn Webster focuses on the ways in which African American parents advocated on behalf of their children's education in Boston, New York, and Philadelphia.[8]

This emphasis on education was not limited to Black women, and AME ministers and bishops promoted the creation of schools wherever churches sprang up. As Stephen W. Angell and Anthony B. Pinn demonstrate in *Social Protest Thought in the African Methodist Episcopal Church, 1862–1939*, the denomination viewed education as the means "to train good Christian citizens who would serve their immediate church community, as well as the larger society."[9] Angell and Pinn's volume includes fourteen essays that originally appeared in the *Review* and that reflect the era's range of concerns: normal/industrial versus classical/higher education; the education of women; the teaching profession; integrated versus Black-only institutions; the teaching of Black studies; and suitable reading material for extrainstitutional study.

The *Review*'s treatment of education mirrored not only larger discussions in the Black press but also the editors' priorities. Though Benjamin T. Tanner served as editor for just four of the forty years covered in this study (1884–88), yet 20 percent of the articles on education appeared during his tenure. During Levi J. Coppin's eight years as editor (1888–96), he published 40 percent of the articles on the topic. Consequently, 60 percent of the articles on education appeared during the first twelve years of the period. During the four years of Hightower T. Kealing's first term as editor (1896–1900), only ten education-related articles appeared, and references to the subject continued to decline over the remaining twelve years of his tenure, when twenty-two articles were published. Finally, Reverdy C. Ransom oversaw the publication of fewer than a dozen articles on education between 1912 and 1924.

Several factors contributed to this shift. Racial uplift proved a central theme during the *Review*'s early years, and articles such as G. M. Elliott's "We Must Educate" (October 1884), S. T. Mitchell's "Is Education Generic?" (July 1885), and Frances Ellen Watkins Harper's "A Factor in Human Progress" (July 1885) address the need for education to ensure the progress of the race. In addition, Booker T. Washington's work at Tuskegee provoked a great deal of reaction in this early period, including such articles as D. Augustus Straker's "The Advantage of Beginning Trades in Our Schools and Colleges" (July 1886) and Will M. Jackson's "Industrial Education the Need of Our Youth" (July 1888). As W. E. B. Du Bois's work at Atlanta University garnered attention in the waning years of the nineteenth century, a series of articles addressed the debate regarding vocational versus classical education: W. V. Tunnell's "The Necessity of Higher Education" (October 1889), W. L. Brown's "The Value of a Classical Education" (January 1892), J. E. Carter's "Is Higher Education Advantageous to the Negro?" (October 1895), E. L. Blackshear's "Lines of Negro Education" (January 1897), and A. D. Delaney, "Higher or Industrial Education—Which Shall It Be?" (April 1899).

Kealing tenure marked the first time the quarterly's editor possessed an academic rather than ecclesiastical background. Kealing had served in a variety of positions in Texas educational institutions, among them Paul Quinn College in Waco, Prairie View State Normal School, and the Austin city schools (April 1909, 383). Kealing steered the *Review* in a new direction: his definition of "educational" material inclined more toward the practical (actual courses of study and curricula) than to the philosophical (the Washington–Du Bois debates), leading to the publication of articles such as William H. Dammond's "Engineering Courses for our Colleges and Universities" (January 1899) and George M. Lightfoot's "The Function of Language in the Secondary and the Higher Education" (April 1900).

Beginning in July 1905, Kealing utilized the *Review*'s "Education" department to offer a new recurring feature, "The Disciplinary Course of Study," that functioned as a kind of correspondence course for those interested in learning the AME denomination's core beliefs as outlined in *The Doctrine and Discipline of the African Methodist Episcopal Church*.[10] Each issue contained instructional material followed by a series of questions; the answers appeared in the following issue, along with another installment of instructional material. The column continued intermittently through 1908.

Kealing's successor, Ransom, was not an academic: he described himself as the "Preacher-Editor" and pointed to his twenty-seven years of service as an itinerant preacher (July 1912, 81). Reflecting his focus on Social Gospel, he declared that he would publish "no commonplace essays on hackneyed or profitless themes" but rather would feature material reflecting "our own appeal for political and social justice in the United States" ("81). Some education-themed articles continued to appear during his time in office, among them contributions from Booker T. Washington ("Industrial Education and Negro Progress" [January 1913]), Josephine J. Turpin Washington ("A Plea for the Moral Aim in Education" [October 1921]), and former Wilberforce University president William S. Scarborough (William S. Scarborough, "The College-Bred Negro" [July 1921]).

The women contributors were teachers at a variety of types of institutions in both the North and the South. As Fairclough observes, the inclusion of the word *university* in an institution's name reflected its founders' aspirations rather than the degrees initially offered, and "most of the pupils who attended the innumerable 'academies,' institutes,' and 'colleges' that flourished between the 1880s and 1920s studied at the elementary level." Instructors generally received their training at normal schools, as institutions that prepared elementary- and secondary-level teachers were called. That training itself often consisted of little more than elementary or secondary education, particularly at normal schools that served African Americans, who were generally educated separately from whites.[11] As Carole Wylie Hancock has noted, at the local level, teachers typically needed to fulfill just two requirements: "earning a locally determined, passing score on a test of content knowledge and pedagogy, and evidence of good moral character."[12]

Mary Elizabeth Lewis Lambert, who contributed "A Bunch of Pansies" (October 1884) *Review*, was an educator who operated first a select school and later a Sunday school. Born in Cincinnati, Ohio, on August 8, 1842, she moved with her family to Toronto as a child and by 1867 had married Toussaint L'Ouverture Lambert and was living in Detroit, Michigan, where they operated a select school (likely a private day school). A decade later, Mollie Lambert was a teacher at an AME-sponsored Sunday school, while her husband served as its superintendent. Over the next decade-plus, she became a well-known Detroit clubwoman, hosting receptions for college graduates, sponsoring the Young People's Missionary and Literary Society, and editing its publication, *The Missionary Chronicle*.[13]

"A Bunch of Pansies" evidently was not Lambert's first publication for the *Review*: according to an article in *The Christian Recorder*, Lambert had published a poem, "My Dream," in the January 1884 issue of the *Review*.[14] "A Bunch of Pansies" appeared in response to Tanner's query, "In your experience of teaching, which of the race element do you find as being the more intelligent of conception and of natural ability?" (October 1884, 150). Noting that she had been educated alongside white students and was accustomed to attending commencement exercises in which the Black valedictory address received "thunderous applause," Lambert observes that she had previously given little thought to this question but that a recent article in the *Review* had caused her to consider the extent to which African Americans possessed "a degree of intellectual capacity equal with the

Caucasian in science, art and literature" (150, 151).[15] Using analogies to the mixture of the colors of the spectrum that produces light and to the beauty in a bunch of pansies of varying hues, Lambert argues that the commingling of the races produces positive results (151–52).

Lambert then goes on to assert that "women are the educators of the world" and that "many fine writers" are found "among those engaged in teaching" (152). The fledgling *Review* might well serve as a vehicle for "exchange of thought" between women writers as well as men (152). Insisting that there is nothing "unloveable, unwomanly, or strong-minded" in an educated woman, Lambert urges women to use their intellect "to the *fullest possible* extent" (152, 153). She further asserts that struggling to achieve education can help young people become more appreciative of it. Lambert details educational efforts among African Americans in Boston, New York, and Philadelphia before noting that after Detroit's Black parents persuaded the public school system to accept their children, those children "stood *side and side equal* in all respects with their *white classmates*, except in such instances where they proved themselves superior" (155). Lambert thus answers Tanner's question by declaring the superiority of Black students, adding that the family and the church must work together with educators to achieve these ends (156). Lambert concludes by observing that the *Review* deserves widespread support as "an outlet for Negro Scholarship" and a chronicler of Black history (157).

Three other Black women working as teachers at the primary/elementary level also contributed to the quarterly during this era, and their stories reflect the life choices available at the time. Hannah Jones, like most women teachers, gave up her career in the public schools when marriage and children intervened.[16] Belle B. Dorce continued to teach Sunday school after her marriage. And Nellie Freeman never married and continued her career in the public schools for the remainder of her life.

Hannah Jones was an 1878 graduate of Philadelphia's Institute for Colored Youth, where she studied under Fanny Jackson Coppin, and received a prize for her article on "Wontan's Kingdom." Jones's degree from the institute was the equivalent of a high school diploma, but it enabled her to obtain a teaching position in her hometown, Freehold, New Jersey, where she remained for ten years. She then returned to Philadelphia and became principal of the Western District Colored School, located at Seventh and Catharine Streets. Jones held that post for about two decades, until around the time of her marriage to the Reverend Howard D. Brown.[17]

When Jones's "Women as Educators" appeared in the April 1893 issue of the *Review*, she would have been around thirty years old and would have had fifteen years' experience teaching in Black public schools. She opens by railing against a man who admitted that "properly trained" women could be competent to practice medicine but nevertheless opined that "God never intended" them to become physicians, an attitude Jones labels "blind, blind prejudice!" (322). She believes that women should educate other women to enter the professions but notes that doing so requires women to be admitted to institutions of higher education (323). She also supports industrial education, which has opened doors for women to become bookkeepers and typists, and praises the Young Women's Christian Association for starting extension classes for women in these areas (324). And Jones argues that women excel as Christian educators "of the soul," pointing to reformers' efforts in prisons and children's homes (326). In short, no level of education should be off-limits.

Like Jones, Freeman had already had a long career as teaching in primary schools by the time her article, "The Duties of a Primary Teacher and How to Perform Them," appeared in the October 1908 issue of the *Review*. She and her sister, Jane H. Freeman, had opened a school on Prospect Street in Cleveland in 1872, and the unmarried sisters continued to live on Prospect Street as late as 1891.[18] In 1908, Freeman likely held some kind of supervisory role in the Cleveland school system, since her work "often" required her to visit Sunday schools (35). She kept up with the contemporary literature on teaching, mentioning the work of noted teacher and author Mary Peabody Mann (Horace Mann's wife) and psychologist G. Stanley

Hall as well as reporting on a recent Sunday school convention in New England (33–36). In Freeman's view, primary school teachers had two equally important tasks, teaching students and molding their character (37), and that at this level a Sunday school is most important because "there the foundations of our religious selves is laid" (34). She also asserts that students who feel loved will strive to excel and offers teaching tips that include using blackboards to hold students' attention (39). Finally, Freeman urges teachers to avoid debating generalized methods of teaching and instead to consider context, choosing whatever method is best suited for a particular lesson in a particular class (37).

Dorce, in contrast, served only a short stint as a teacher in Lebanon, Ohio. Born in Bowling Green, Kentucky, on September 15, 1867, Dorce graduated from Lincoln Institute in Jefferson City, Missouri, a few months after her September 1886 marriage to the Reverend Solomon George Dorce. In addition to her July 1887 *Review* article, "The New Education," Dorce contributed writings to *The Christian Recorder*. She died in 1891, when she was just twenty-three.[19]

Dorce's six years of study at Lincoln Institute apparently included significant exposure to the latest trends in education, and "The New Education" demonstrates a wide-ranging knowledge of instructional methods. Dorce begins by tracing the origins of the word *educate* to the Latin *educere*, which she defines as "to lead or draw out" (509). She continues with the observation that many people respond to "new" methods simply by denouncing them but goes on to discuss beneficial educational innovations that go beyond rote learning to stress the "harmonious development of the entire being" (510). Dorce applauds the introduction of the kindergarten for children between ages three and seven (510). She then critiques some specific educational approaches: the "Quincy Method" is good in some respects but goes too far in urging the elimination of textbooks, but she does not recommend the "Grube Method," which focuses on teaching through a number system (510). Dorce comments approvingly on Francis Wayland Parker's fourfold system, which advocates

(1) training children in nature, allowing them to explore; (2) eschewing rote repetition; (3) avoiding un-sought-after knowledge; and (4) teaching the principle of Christian love as the foundation for learning and happiness (511). In Dorce's view, merely training the "intellect" is not enough: training the mind, the body, and the soul will produce the best results (510).

Frances Ellen Watkins Harper (see chapter 4) contributed a July 1885 *Review* article that responded to G. M. Elliott's "We Must Educate," which appeared in the April 1885 issue. In "A Factor in Human Progress," Harper argues that "the education of the intellect and the training of the morals must go hand in hand" (14).[20] She adds that the question ought not to be "What will education do for us? but What will it help us to do for others?" (15). Harper embraces a philosophy of self-sacrifice that she traces back to Moses, Buddha, the Roman Curtius, the Greek Theseus, and Christ, declaring that "self-sacrifice and self-surrender have been the golden cords that have lifted men nearer to God, and brought heaven closer to earth" (16–17). Sidestepping the question of how African Americans should be educated, Harper focuses on the ultimate goal: "What a field of usefulness lies before the educated young men and women of our race!" (18).

Josephine J. Turpin Washington's many contributions to the *Review* include three articles that concern education: "A Plea for the Co-Education of the Sexes" (January 1887), "Teaching as a Profession" (October 1888), and "A Plea for the Moral Aim in Education" (October 1921).[21] Although recognized by scholars primarily as a pioneering Black journalist, Washington also served as a teacher throughout much of her career, including stints at Selma University (1888–89), Tuskegee Institute (1893–96), and Lincoln Normal School (1900–1913). As Gloria Wade-Gayles notes, early Black women journalists rarely received compensation for their writing and consequently often supported themselves by working as teachers. In addition to the *Review*, Washington's work appeared in *The Virginia Star*, *The Industrial Herald*, *The Planet*, *The New York Globe*, *The New York Freeman*, and *The Christian Recorder*.[22]

Washington's Howard University degree made her much more highly educated than most of her peers, and "A Plea for the Co-Education of the Sexes" makes the case that women should receive greater access to higher education. To support her contention that "the advantages of co-education far outnumber its disadvantages," she asserts that coeducation is "natural" because young boys and girls are initially educated by their mothers and because "those who are destined to live together are surely right in thus learning together" (267, 268). She counters the belief that women require only the education suitable for marriage and motherhood by declaring that a classical education teaches both men and women the "power to acquire and think" and that "there can be no mission requiring a more thorough development of all the thinking faculties than that of wifehood and motherhood" (268). Moreover, she contends, coeducation is demoralizing only when it is mismanaged, a friendly rivalry benefits both sexes, and constant interaction stimulates "greater neatness" and "proper personal pride" for both men and women (270). Finally, Washington cites statistics and opinions from the US Bureau of Education on the "universality" of coeducation's benefits (270).

Washington's arguments regarding the value of a broader education are echoed by other contributors, including two who stressed the importance of music and the arts. Mattie F. Roberts, author of "Which Is the More Useful Art—Painting or Music?" (January 1887), was born in Adrian, Michigan, and graduated from Adrian College with a degree in music in 1885. After serving as a music teacher in the Lansing, Michigan, city schools, she taught music, art, and oil painting at Wilberforce University. Roberts, who never married, subsequently taught in the Indianapolis city schools for thirty-five years prior to her 1936 death.[23]

To answer her article's title question, Roberts asserts that music is ubiquitous, appearing throughout nature—in thunder, in babbling brooks, in birdsong, and in the human voice—whereas painting constitutes an "imitation" of the beauties of nature, secondary rather than primary to the senses (295). While God has bestowed artistic abilities on every human, music touches the heart and soul of everyone who encounters it (296, 297). She therefore concludes that music is more useful than painting as an aid to moral and religious education (297).

While Roberts was teaching art and music in Wilberforce's University Division, Sarah C. Bierce Scarborough (see chapter 1) was teaching industrial drawing in the school's Normal Department. Her article "Music in Education" (January 1902) discusses the evolution of music in ancient Greek and Roman curricula. Scarborough notes that the Greeks were the first to teach music as a science, incorporating it into a curriculum that offered gymnastics to train the body and music to train the soul (218). Music combined with poetry thus formed the "starting point" of all subsequent education, out of which the arts and sciences grew (218). The Romans continued to teach music but "initiated nothing," merely borrowing from the Greek and Egyptian cultures (220). Scarborough disagrees with the idea that "music is a universal language," noting that tastes vary widely and citing the Chinese tom-tom and Egyptian cow horn flute as producing sounds that others may have difficulty understanding and appreciating (221). Nevertheless, she believes that music has a place alongside more "practical" courses in the curriculum because "life is more than mere existence" and music is emblematic of the "beautiful and the good" (223).

The *Review*'s women contributors on the subject of education used their experience as teachers to push the discussion beyond the Washington–Du Bois debates to encompass issues such as coeducation and integrated education. As in other areas, these authors generally grounded their arguments in pious feminism, stressing women's role as the first educators of their children and framing that role as an outgrowth of women's Christian calling to be useful servants of society.

CHAPTER 7

Matters Scientific and Philosophical

As Britt Rusert notes in *Fugitive Science: Empiricism and Freedom in Early African American Culture*, "The very definition of science was capacious and flexible in early to mid-nineteenth-century contexts, and neither science nor medicine was professionalized in the United States until later in the nineteenth century."[1] Consequently, the relatively few "scientific" and "philosophical" articles in the *A.M.E. Church Review* from this period reflect fairly fluid conceptions of those fields.

However, women were nearly as likely as men to author those contributions. Male authors tended to contribute more philosophical essays, perhaps as a result of what both the writers and editors expected their audience of predominantly AME members might most appreciate, and scientific articles primarily sought to bring findings into conversation with biblical teachings. This category includes three of the seven original articles submitted by men during this period: "The Harmony Between the Bible and Science Concerning Primitive Man" (Prof. D. B. Williams, July 1892); "Science Confirming the Scriptures" (Albert B. Cooper, July 1899); and "Is There a Conflict Between Religion and Science?" (Rev. J. N. Goddard, October 1924). As with articles on education, women's contributions tended more toward the practical (for example, Josephine Silone Yates's "Natural Science in the Schools" [July 1889] and "Physiology and Hygiene" [April 1890] and Hallie Tanner Dillon's "Practical Physiology" [October 1892]).

Science

During the editorship of Hightower T. Kealing, the Science/Scientific Department provided consistent coverage of the topic, though it generally consisted of excerpts from other publications. These excerpts tended to reflect the sorts of practical concerns about which the women contributors wrote—overall health, food safety, and disease treatment and prevention.[2] When Reverdy C. Ransom succeeded Kealing, scientific articles virtually disappeared from the quarterly; those that did appear generally were book reviews in the "Within the Sphere of Letters" column, which first appeared in October 1912 and was curated by George W. Forbes of the Boston Public Library.

Between 1884 and 1894, the *Review* published six lengthy articles by R. K. Potter, the nom de plume of Josephine Silone Yates (see chapter 2). Three ("Land of the Czar" [October 1888], "Russia's New Literature" [January 1889], and "Natural Science in the Schools" [July 1889]) appeared prior to her 1889 marriage. She published three more pseudonymous works over the next three years ("Physiology and Hygiene" [April 1890], "The Educators of Literary Taste" [April 1891], and "Theosophy and the Theosophical School" [October 1892]) before dropping her pen name. While some women contributors employed pseudonyms to disguise the fact that they had contributed other material in the same issue, Yates does not appear to have been motivated by this consideration, and it seems likely that her husband encouraged her to publish under her full name.

By the time "Natural Science in the Schools" appeared in the *Review*, Yates had already spent several years as head of the science department at the Lincoln Institute in Jefferson City, Missouri. The article opens by honoring the work of Enlightenment educators such as Bacon, Rousseau, Locke, and Spencer as well as the scientific discoveries of Copernicus, Newton, Faraday, Dalton, and Agassiz (16–17). Yates then asks, "Of what use is the study of natural science in the schools?" (17). In addition to the "material good" resulting from scientific findings (electric lights, the telegraph, the telephone, transoceanic cables), she argues, science contributes to "mental growth" and to the "moral or physical well-being of man" (18). Yates advocates a graduated curriculum that stimulates student curiosity in the elementary grades and then encourages observation and independent research in the secondary grades and high school (21). Elementary and secondary students should learn physiology, botany, zoology, mineralogy, and geology, with physics, chemistry, biology, and astronomy reserved for high school students. Yates concludes by observing that because very few students attend college, high schools should emphasize the practical applications of science.

In "Physiology and Hygiene" Yates references her earlier contribution and explains, "We now wish to show that, from a long list of these subjects taught under the heading of Natural Science, there are none which have more practical bearing upon the public welfare than the study of Physiology and Hygiene" (411). Elementary students need to understand basic anatomy (structures and forms) as well as physiology ("knowledge of the organs and their function") and hygiene ("conditions of health and disease"), which is important for preventing illness and producing the conditions for long life (412). Citing life expectancy rates among European countries and the United States, she argues that those countries with the highest developments in "sanitary science" also offer the greatest longevity to their citizens (413). She declares "physical culture" as key to disease prevention, linking the Greeks' efforts in systematizing exercise and gymnastics to their advancements in science and the arts (415). Yates advocates a regimen of "exercise, sleep, air, food, and bathing" as the hallmark of good hygiene and argues that increasing physical activity improves "mental power" and contributes to "the formation of character" (415–17). Yates concludes by noting that the stresses of modern society lead to "nervous exhaustion" and the use of "stimulants and narcotics," including alcohol, by both adults and youth (418). She advises educators in the public schools to avoid increasing the pressure on students by balancing mental exertion with a strong grounding in physiology and hygiene (420).

Eager to showcase the race's educational attainments, *Review* editors published articles submitted by Black women who obtained medical training despite the challenges of doing so. As Darlene Clark Hine asserts in "Co-Laborers in the Work of the Lord: Nineteenth-Century Black Women Physicians," two factors that assisted women in overcoming these hurdles were "family background and prior education," and two of the women she profiles, Hallie Tanner Dillon and Susan Smith McKinney, both fit that pattern and contributed articles to the *Review*.[3]

Dillon's October 1892 article, "Practical Physiology," is the first submitted by a woman physician. Hallie E. Tanner was born on October 17, 1864, to AME bishop Benjamin T. Tanner and Sarah Elizabeth Miller Tanner. She married Charles E. Dillon in 1886; had a daughter, Sadie, in 1888, and was widowed by the time she graduated from Woman's Medical College of Pennsylvania on May 6, 1891. She became the first woman to earn a medical license in Alabama after passing the state's grueling ten-day test and earning the highest average in her group, and served as the resident physician at Tuskegee Normal and Industrial School. She subsequently married the Reverend John Quincy Johnson and had three sons (John Quincy Johnson, Benjamin Tanner Johnson, and Henry T. Johnson) prior to her death on April 26, 1901, likely as a result of complications from childbirth.[4]

"Practical Physiology" was the transcript of an address given before the Alabama Teachers Association. According to Dillon, Black citizens had higher birth rates than their white counterparts between 1860 and 1880, but higher death rates among the race meant that population growth favored white Americans (184). Moreover, although some white physicians believed that white citizens healed better after suffering injuries or undergoing surgery, anecdotal evidence suggests that Black patients healed at least as well (185). Nonetheless, inadequate housing, insufficient food supplies, and unsanitary living conditions rendered African Americans more susceptible to certain illnesses, particularly tuberculosis (187). Dillon attributes the existence of such conditions to general ignorance of practical physiology, which could be overcome by persistent and consistent instruction in the home and school as well as the incorporation of physical exercise into the daily curriculum, thereby reducing the number of premature African American deaths (186, 187).

Susan Maria Smith was born sometime between 1840 and 1848 and graduated from the New York Medical School for Women and Children in 1870, received postgraduate training at Long Island College Hospital, and became the state's first Black female doctor. She was practicing medicine in Brooklyn by 1872, around the time of her marriage to the Reverend William G. McKinney. McKinney died on November 24, 1894, and she married the Reverend Theophilus Gould Steward two years later. At the peak of her career, she staffed two Brooklyn offices, founded the Woman's Loyal Union, served on the board of managers for the Brooklyn Home for Aged Colored People, and was active in the Kings County Homeopathic Society. Following her retirement from her medical career, she and her husband joined the faculty at Wilberforce University, and she remained there until her death on March 7, 1918.[5]

McKinney's article, "Marasmus Infantum" (April 1887), focused on a practical application of science—the treatment of marasmus (chronic undernourishment), which was common among her Brooklyn child patients. According to McKinney, as a Black woman trained in homeopathic rather than traditional ("allopathic") medical care, she faced "prejudice against sex, race and school" when starting her practice (424). She explains to readers the disease is commonly associated with unsuitable food, chronic vomiting or diarrhea, worms, "and more especially by inherited syphilis" (425). Treatment depends largely on the disease's causes and severity, and "the prognosis is most unfavorable" when syphilis is involved, but in other instances, her patients have recovered (424, 425). After suggesting various food alternatives, particularly for infants who are having difficulty nursing, she concludes her article suggesting that other doctors share accounts of successful treatments for other childhood illnesses (425), though no such articles appeared.

Mamie Jarvis contributed a general article on "Health" that was printed in the April 1896 *Review*.[6] "The state of being sound in body and in mind," health demands "firmness of muscle," soundness of digestion, adequate sleep, abstinence from alcoholic beverages, and avoidance of colds (516–18). Jarvis recommends "walking, running, boating" to maintain firm musculature, a likely indicator that she imagined her audience to be men and women with leisure time rather than members of the laboring classes (517). She recommends "plain and wholesome" foods, noting that Scottish peasants thrive on oatmeal and milk, Zulus follow a diet of milk and cracked maize, and many of the world's people subsist on a steady diet of rice (517–18). Jarvis's endorsement of Anglo-Saxon king Alfred the Great's recommendation that each day include eight hours of work, eight hours of recreation, and eight hours of rest (518) again indicates that she saw her readers as members of the middle and upper classes. She chides "young Americans" for eating too much meat and too many sweets, noting that indigestion related to such a diet can lead to a host of other ills, including a "bad temper and sullen disposition" (518). Jarvis concludes by asking "Is it a duty to be healthy?" and answering in the affirmative: bodies are given by "our Maker" for our "use, not abuse," and Christians have a duty to maintain their health so that they can minister to the needs of others (519).

Ruth Brinson, author of "The Powerful Influence of Heredity, Its Effect upon Individuals and Races" (January 1895), was the fifth of eight children born to James F. and Louisa Brinson, who were originally from Mississippi. The family settled in Xenia, Ohio, where Brinson likely attended Wilberforce University before moving southeast to the village of Jamestown and opening "Miss Brinson's School" sometime before 1891. On August 9, 1896, she spoke to an audience at St. John's AME Church in Xenia regarding her involvement with the Christian Endeavor movement. She was teaching in Jamestown's African American high school by 1898, the same year she contributed several articles to *The Christian Recorder* in which she provided young women with advice for finding teaching positions after completing high school or college. When the Jamestown High School integrated around the turn of the century, Brinson continued to teach there. On July 18, 1903, Brinson married Winston A. Gales, a farmer from Cedarville, Ohio, and the subsequently moved to Evansville, Indiana, and then to Wilberforce, Ohio. Winston Gales sued for divorce in November 1918, and Ruth Brinson Gales went on to teach in public schools in North Carolina and New York before returning to Xenia, where she died in 1960.[7]

Brinson's article demonstrates that she was highly influenced by theories of heredity that blamed parents for the sins and foibles of their offspring, and she paints a grim picture. She argues that although parents' physical features are commonly recognized in children, "we" fail to recognize that parents' moral failings also play a role in the development of their offspring's character (403–5). "Tendencies" develop into "habits," and a man's youthful tendencies, even if successfully curbed, may curse his son, giving the example of a young man who works in a saloon and many years later finds himself an old man weeping beside the grave of his drunkard son even though his marriage to "a good Christian woman" reformed him and his children never saw him take a drink (408). Although she claims that she is "not fond of dark pictures," Brinson provides several similar ominous anecdotes, portraying young women as frivolous and useless and young men as impure and dissolute (412–14). In her view, learned men should "cease to measure the distance of heavenly bodies" and instead "teach the people the power of heredity" (413), reflecting some of the deterministic pseudoscientific theories that were popular at the time.

Yates's later *Review* essays published under her own name display her knowledge of the geographical sciences. Her two-part essay, "River Systems of the United States" (January 1894, April 1894) provides an overview not only of US geography but also of the federal government agencies that assist in the regulation and preservation of the nation's waterways. By declaring that "great aeons of geologic time" (April 1894, 508) had been necessary for the formation of these river systems, Yates presents a scientific challenge to the Creation as depicted in Genesis. She traces water from rills formed in mountains to rivulets (gatherings of rills) to torrents cascading down mountains to rivers where the terrain levels off (January 1894, 349). Yates further distinguishes between the upper, middle, and lower courses of rivers and describes the four natural divisions of US rivers: the Great Basin (between Rocky Mountains and the Mississippi), the Pacific Ocean (west of the Rockies), the Atlantic Ocean (east of the Appalachians), and the Gulf of Mexico (between the Mississippi and the Appalachians) (351–53).

Part 2 of Yates's article opens with a discussion of immature versus mature rivers and distinguishes between tidal and tideless rivers (April 1894, 509). She observes that the government has spent large sums of money on largely unsuccessful attempts to deepen the channels of the Mississippi (510). Yates reminds readers rail travel has not yet replaced river traffic and that transcontinental railways follow riverbeds (513–14). She also notes that irrigation provided by the great rivers erased the "Great Desert" found on early maps of the American West, crediting the US Geological Survey for "bringing forth scientific methods" to manage land and water, and the US Fish Commission for promoting "artificial fish culture" by seeding rivers and lakes to increase food production (515). Finally, she reminds readers of the importance of clean water for urban residents' health and expresses her hope that additional "scientific study" might yield "commensurate returns" (516).

In "Municipal Franchises" (April 1895), Yates discusses the pros and cons of granting individuals and corporations franchises for public improvements such as parks, waterworks, railways, and electric lighting. After reviewing the history of municipal franchises as far back as feudal days, she explains that the process may advance city development but can also lead to corruption. She urges American cities to follow the lead of London, Birmingham, and Glasgow in Great Britain by hiring workers to expand and maintain such facilities and thereby avoid allowing mayors to award contracts to cronies (442–44). She holds up Chicago as a cautionary tale, arguing that its uneven development—a block of paved streets and sidewalks followed by a block of mud and grazing cows—demonstrates the need for more direct city control (447). That said, she admits that the rapid growth of many western cities and the difficulty of finding buyers for city bonds may necessitate the continued use of municipal franchises (448). However, Yates argues, a state is a "political entity" while the city is a "more business organization," and should be run on sound business principles (448–49). She concludes with the hope that twentieth-century American cities will resemble those envisioned by Edward Bellamy in his utopian novel *Looking Backward* (449).

"Rural Versus Urban," the lead article in the April 1912 quarterly, is a review of John Bookwalter's 1911 volume, *Rural Versus Urban, Their Conflict and Its Causes*, which Yates identifies as a "scientific inquiry" into increasingly high prices for necessary goods—"i.e., of the cost of living" (735). But it also provides her with a platform from which to opine on current conditions in America. According to Yates, Bookwalter uses Italy as a case study of the origins of "budgetary warfare" between rural and urban areas (735). Italian "hill cities" such as Capua and Rome depended on domestic agriculture for their prosperity and enacted laws that gradually encroached on rural life (737, 740). Bookwalter subsequently cites France as an exemplar for protecting the interests of rural folk by concentrating the "agricultural population into villages and communes," thereby ensuring a source of communal strength and argues that England's disastrous Corn Laws encouraged the concentration of wealth in industrial areas, thereby devastating farmers (741).

But the major "raison d-etre," for Bookwalter's volume, in Yates's view, is his accusation that the United States is even more insidious than England in promoting the transfer of wealth to the cities (741). Overproduction of food from 1870 to 1900 led to increased supply and lower prices, cutting into farmers' earnings and reducing the value of their holdings. The decline in farming profits and increased opportunities available in cities led to a migration from rural to urban areas (743–44). According to Bookwalter's statistics by 1900, three-quarters of the nation's wealth was concentrated in urban areas despite the fact that rural areas retained the majority of the nation's population (745, 746). Yates concludes by applying Bookwalter's lessons to African Americans, positing that Black laborers "barred very largely from the trades and many other remunerative vocations" in the cities should study the possibilities of "intensive farming" or city lot "back yard" farming (747). She further suggests that philanthropists such as Andrew Carnegie might better spend their fortunes on "farm colonies" in the country than on libraries in the cities (747). Writing at the beginning of the Great Migration of African Americans from rural Southern states to Northern cities, Yates embraces a "back to the land" approach for righting America's economic ship.

Philosophy

Kealing never created a specific department for philosophical material, and none of the articles published during his tenure included the words *philosophy* or *philosophical* in the titles. Nonetheless, he and the other editors during this period published material that was philosophical in nature, though the subject, considered a branch of higher education, was largely the realm of male contributors.

Tanner published "The Proverbial Philosophy of the Colored Race" (October 1884) and "An Analysis of Science, Philosophy and Theology" (April 1886), both of which were authored by J. A. M. Jones. The *Review*'s second editor, Levi J. Coppin, published three articles directly addressing philosophy: "Philosophy Religiously Valued" by H. T. Johnson (April 1891); "Creation of the World Opposed to the Theory of Natural Philosophy" by James W. Lavatt (July 1891); and "The Philosophy of Progress" by D. J. Jordan (July 1893).[8] Jones's second article and Lavatt's piece primarily address the conflicts between modern science, religion as taught and practiced by the AME denomination, and "natural philosophy," a term used to refer to the treatment of nature before the birth of modern science.[9]

Late-nineteenth-century college students generally studied philosophy in their final year. The course, particularly in institutions founded by religious denominations, was often taught by the school's president and stressed ethical and theological issues. Even at institutions founded by religious denominations, students frequently received instruction in the classical texts of philosophy, among them works by Plato, Kant, Hegel, and Hume.[10] Elite African American women who attended college or who had access to libraries also formed ideas of a philosophical nature, and some contributed articles on the subject to the *Review*.

Among the four *Review* articles contributed by Frazelia Campbell (see chapter 1), one "The Sixteenth Century in the Education of Modern Thought" (July 1903), had a philosophical topic. Campbell opens the ten-page piece by arguing for a distinct break between the thought and expressions of the fifteenth century and those of the sixteenth (31–32). When Constantinople fell, Greek and Roman learning spread to the west, leading to the birth of modern philosophy and the religious reformation (33). Campbell devotes the bulk of the article to analyzing the contributions of Bacon, Calvin, Knox, Luther, Wesley, Fox, Shakespeare, and others (33–35). In addition, she traces other modern practices to the Renaissance— civic freedoms; international cooperation; modern warfare based on territorial expansion; alongside modern diplomacy; Utopian visions of the future realized in shortened workdays, public libraries, parks, and playgrounds; a spirit of tolerance; expanded educational opportunities; and a revival of scientific inquiry and experimentation (33–40). Campbell closes with a refrain from James Russell Lowell's 1885 *Biglow Papers* (satirical verses written in a Yankee dialect) that undercuts the learned history she has just recited but nevertheless packs a proverbial punch:

> Tell ye jest the eend I've come to,
> Arter Cipherin' plaguey smart,
> An' it makes a handy sum, tu,
> Any gump could larn by heart;
> Laborin' man and laborin' woman
> Hev one glory an' one shame.
> Ev'y thin' that's done inhuman
> Injers all on 'em the same.

Campbell thus demonstrates that a Black woman can master Western (white) philosophical history and its influences on modern thought but undercuts white male pretensions of classical education by concluding with Russell's satirical verse stressing that what is done inhumanely to one person in fact injures all.

Sylvanie Francoz Williams, who contributed "Action for the Hour" (April 1886), was born in 1848. Her father was from France, and her biography presents an interesting case study in the vagaries of racial determination and the inconsistencies in census reporting conducted by white census takers. Both the 1870 and 1880 US Censuses record her as "Mulatto"; however, she is described as "Colored (Black)" in the 1900 Census and as "White" two decades later. An 1881 article describing the commencement ceremonies at New Orleans's Peabody Normal School reports that the hall was "crowded with the most select audience of every shade in the city" and describes Williams both as "one shade below the octoroon" and as "in some respects superior, and others, inferior" to a woman who was "a pure type of the white race." Williams appears to have been well known both locally and across Louisiana. She and her husband, Professor Arthur P. Williams, operated a summer school for Black teachers through the Peabody Normal School, and she served as president of the New Orleans Colored Teachers' League during the 1890s. In 1892, Williams, at the time the principal of the Fisk School for Girls, prepared a detailed report on the status of African American education in the state. She delivered a welcome

FIGURE 7.1. SYLVANIE FRANCOZ WILLIAMS. FROM THE NEW YORK PUBLIC LIBRARY DIGITAL COLLECTIONS.

address at the July 1910 meeting of the Louisiana Negro Business League held in New Orleans and received the governor's appointment to attend the 1916 Southern Sociological Congress, also held in the city. She died in 1921.[11]

Williams's article employs the metaphor of a sculptor chiseling a block of marble to describe the Black race's carving out of its own history (433). Espousing the widely accepted view that "education is the first step" forward for the race, she asserts the need to target students' "intellectual as well as moral" nature (434). Williams believes that although the "Caucasian race" has the advantage of two thousand years of civilization, she reminds readers that their ancestors—the "great men of science" of Abyssinia who calculated the paths of the celestial bodies—have given African Americans all they need to succeed and that they can rely solely on their own efforts in the "slow but sure" process to reach the race's full potential (435–36).

Journalist and teacher Josephine J. Turpin's "A Remedy for War" (October 1887) is both political and philosophical in nature. The author blames the "passions of men" for history's many wars of conquest and advocates substituting "negotiation and arbitration" through the formation of a "Supreme Court of Nations" or "Congress of Nations" that can adjudicate disputes (161–63). These ideas echo an 1840 proposal by William Ladd, an antiwar activist and the first president of the American Peace Society.[12] Turpin adds that the spread of Christianity and "unrestricted commerce" between nations will produce the surest spread of civilization (164). Turpin then points to other instances of arbitration, including the Amphictyonic Council of ancient Greece, the Republican Party's 1884 adoption of a statement advocating "International Arbitration for International Differences," and the AME Church's resolution in support of the "National Arbitration League" (164). She also anticipates and answers objections, such as the cost of forming such a body (wars are more expensive), the danger in giving power to such a tribunal (all nations will assist in drawing up its principles), and the inability to enforce decisions (international bans on trade with such countries would work). How can her readers assist such efforts? "Agitate . . . agitate . . . AGITATE" (165). She then concludes with an Edenic vision of a future world without war "ruled by the heads of the wise and the hearts of the good, rather than by the hands of the proud, the powerful and the despotic" (166).

Another hybrid historical and philosophical article appeared in April 1889. "The Decisions of Time" was written by Julia L. Caldwell, an Alabama native who was raised in Columbus, Georgia, and graduated from Howard University. She later moved to Dallas, Texas, where she served as teacher and later assistant principal of the Colored High School and in 1909 married another teacher, Charles Wales Wellington Frazier. A 1928 article identified her as "one of the foremost female educators of the colored race" as well as "head of the colored House of Ruth of Texas," and following her 1929 death, Dallas named a school in her honor. She is also the namesake of Howard University's first residence hall for women.[13]

Caldwell's piece traces human progress from the Greeks to the final decades of the nineteenth century, noting particularly the ways in which the gradual throwing off of race and caste prejudice has benefited both African Americans and women. She begins by exploring "political" evolution from the "patriarchy" of the Old Testament to "feudalism" to "monarchy" and finally to the establishment of "republics" culminating in the American experience (344). Caldwell next turns to "intellectual" evolution from the art, literature, and science of the ancients through the Dark Ages and into the Reformation (345). She notes that many great philosophers—Socrates, Aristotle, Galileo—were ostracized during their lives and not fully appreciated until after they died (345–46). Like Turpin and others, Caldwell credits the spread of Christianity for improving the treatment of women, who now graduate from colleges and can be found in all of the professions (347). Embracing Charles Darwin's concept of survival of the fittest, she predicts that the Black race will thrive and that "the hydra-headed monsters, caste and race prejudice," will be cut down and "men of all races" will seek the truth together (348).

Noted educator Fanny Jackson Coppin, who under the pseudonym Catherine Casey also served as editor of the "Woman's Department" of *The Christian Recorder*, published very little in the *A.M.E. Church Review*.[14] She participated in symposiums honoring Bishops Jabez Pitt Campbell (October 1891) and Daniel A. Payne (January 1894) and penned "A Field of Golden Grain or a Harvest of Rank Weeds" (January 1901). Taking an agricultural analogy, Coppin points out that just as a farmer who plants corn seeds expects corn to grow and one who plants wheat expects that crop to sprout, individuals' choice of reading materials will impact the quality of their minds (195). Moreover, "mental taste" can be cultivated like taste for any other kind of nourishment (196). She advises readers to begin with the Bible and then consider Bunyan's *Pilgrim's Progress*, both of which old and young alike can understand and enjoy (196). Coppin urges men to fill their pockets with small inspirational volumes that can be used to cultivate the mind between other engagements and recommends the poems of Black authors (197). Coppin urges readers to move on to the classics—the *Iliad*, the *Aeneid*, the *Divine Comedy*, and *Paradise Lost*—and concludes that "what we think entitles us a place among the truly noble of the earth and an everlasting home with the pure in heart in heaven" (198).

Among the few philosophical essays published during Ransom's tenure, Edna Dredden Gullins's combination of reportage, history, and philosophy stands out. Born around 1892, Gullins was married to the Reverend William R. Gullins, who served nearly a dozen Pennsylvania congregations during his career. Edna Gullins became a leader in church, community, national, and international organizations, among them AME missionary societies, the Interracial Department of the Philadelphia Council of Churches, and the Women's International League for Peace and Freedom. A sought-after speaker, Gullins also contributed to *The Christian Recorder*, wrote poetry, and authored a three-part novella, "Those Other People," that appeared in the January, April, and July 1920 issues of the *Review*.[15]

The seeds of Gullins's commitment to the league (founded in 1915 in The Hague, Netherlands, as the International Women's Congress) may have been sown earlier than the events described in her article, "At Gettysburg" (July 1922).[16] Following the AME Church's annual conference in Chambersburg, Pennsylvania, several participants, including the presiding bishop, toured the historic battlefield at Gettysburg, where a group of young white soldiers jeered at them. According to Gullins, church members' response to being "denied the common courtesy" given to even the "unnaturalized peasantry of another country" "far exceeded bitterness" (33). Fifty-nine years after the Battle of Gettysburg, her people still lacked true liberty and had to continue to fight, though the race's "weapons of warfare" were now spiritual in nature. She urges readers to "temper justice with mercy, to suppress bitterness with brotherly love and understanding" (34). Bowing her head at the statue of Lincoln at Gettysburg, however, Gullins calls out white Americans for their injustices: "They segregate, they persecute, they discriminate, they lynch, but we've paid our vow to the Lord and we won't turn back" (34). Borrowing from Lincoln's Gettysburg Address, she concludes with the hope "that government of the people, for the people, by the people shall not perish from the earth" (34).

Conclusion
Writing Race Literature in Extraordinary Times

The published writings of Edna Dredden Gullins, like those of many of the women contributors to the *A.M.E. Church Review* between 1884 and 1924, remain underexamined in the scholarly literature—primarily as a consequence of the lack of access to the religious periodicals in which those writings appeared. As is the case for the *Review*, few issues of contemporaneous publications from other Black denominations—*The Star of Zion* (African Methodist Episcopal Zion), *The National Baptist Union-Review* (National Baptist Convention), and *The Christian Index* (Colored Methodist Episcopal)—are available digitally; most exist on microfilm or in print at scattered institutions. Yet recovering these writings is vital to achieving a more capacious understanding of the development of Black print culture and particularly of those publications, like the *Review*, whose editors responded to Victoria Earle Matthews's call for a developing "race literature." Recovering these materials also proves vital for understanding women's contributions to Black intellectual history as well as the centrality of Black women's voices in the myriad reform movements of the Progressive Era.

Women contributors to the *Review* aggressively supported and wrote about many of the social issues of their time, among them education, temperance, suffrage, child welfare, and prison reform.

Many of these women became social activists through their local churches, women's clubs, and regional and national organizations. Their contributions to the *Review* educated others about issues of concern to African American citizens. Their contributions included not only traditional literary matter—poetry, fiction, drama—but also prose essays across a wide variety of themes and genres: literary criticism, history, biography, sociology, travel writing, and education, scientific, and philosophical discourses. They helped to realize Matthews's goal and to fulfill Hightower T. Kealing's pledge to move beyond the *Review*'s previous focus on theological subject matter.

Moreover, these women lived in extraordinary times: some had been born into slavery and lived through the Civil War and Reconstruction. Others learned to read and write in the schools for African Americans that proliferated in the last half of the nineteenth century—Sunday schools, select schools, public schools, academies, normal schools, colleges, and universities. Part of W. E. B. Du Bois's "Talented Tenth," many contributors were teachers who brought literacy to their communities or pursued other careers in the helping professions. Some saw their fathers, brothers, husbands, and sons serve in the Spanish-American War and World War I. Some became part of the Great Migration, either moving themselves in search of a better life or welcoming fellow African Americans to the North.

And at the same time, many of these women raised families and supported minister husbands during an era when the AME Church relied primarily on an itinerant preaching model, moving men from parish to parish every few years.[1] AME churchwomen were expected to raise funds to support local ministers and to construct church buildings and parsonages, to teach in Sunday schools and community-sponsored schools, and to serve in church-sponsored missionary societies. But the denomination's patriarchal leadership structure always restricted them to secondary roles, circumscribing the path these women navigated in balancing the demands of their Christian faith, their loyalty to their husbands, and their desire not merely to uplift the race but to uplift their African American sisters.

While it is likely that none of the women contributors would have claimed the mantle of feminist, they clearly viewed their publications as opportunities to advocate on behalf of expanded opportunities for African American women, doing so from the position of pious feminism. Many others—either with or without formal academic training in the emerging fields of social work or sociology—engaged in feminized sociology, contributing their time, talents, and resources to combating a variety of social ills.

Future scholarly work on the *Review* might be enhanced by improved access to demographic data for African Americans born in the nineteenth century and, where necessary, additional creative speculation about the lives of women difficult to locate in the archives. It might also include analysis of poetry, fiction, and drama, especially from lesser-known women contributors. It might also include a deeper investigation of pseudonymous submissions, which could help to determine other contributions from women writers. And sustained exploration of the material in the departments initiated by Kealing—Women, Educational, Business, Miscellaneous, for example—might also prove fruitful. Scholars of Black religion—particularly of the history of the African Methodist Episcopal Church and its sister Methodist denominations, African Methodist Episcopal Zion and Colored Methodist Episcopal—might compare matter published in the *Review* with that found in other denominational periodicals. Finally, attention to the *Review*'s visual material might interest art historians and scholars of visual communication. There is still much scholars can learn from these long-overlooked sources.

Appendix
Women Contributors and Their Articles in the "A.M.E. Church Review," 1884-1924

Name	Article Title	Issue
Anderson, Mrs. Willam T.	Symposium on Temperance	April 1891
Bentley, Fannie C.	"The Women of Our Race Worthy of Imitation"	April 1890
Bragg, Lucinda B.	"Music, and Woman's Relation to It"	April 1887
Brinson, Ruth	"The Powerful Influence of Heredity, Its Effect upon Individuals and Races"	January 1895
Caldwell, Julia L.	"The Decisions of Time"	April 1889
Campbell, Frazelia	"Die Beiden Piccolomini"	January 1885
	"Tacitus' German Women"	July 1885
	"Milton's Satan"	October 1890
	"The Sixteenth Century in the Education of Modern Thought"	July 1903
Carter, E. Marie	"Notes of Travel"	1903–12
Chappelle, Rosina	"Women as Helpers of the Ministers in the Spiritual and Social Activities of the Church"	April 1913

Coppin, Fanny Jackson	Symposium in Honor of Bishop Jabez Pitt Campbell	October 1891
	Symposium in Honor of Bishop Daniel A. Payne	January 1894
	"A Field of Golden Grain or a Harvest of Rank Weed"	January 1901
Dillon, Hallie Tanner	"Practical Physiology"	October 1892
Dorce, Belle B.	"The New Education"	July 1887
Earle, Victoria	"The Crispus Attucks Monument"	April 1889
Frazier, Susan Elizabeth	"Some Afro-American Women of Mark"	April 1892
Freeman, Nellie	"The Duty of a Primary Teacher and How to Perform It"	October 1908
Gullins, Edna Dredden	"At Gettysburg"	July 1922
Hackley, Azalia E.	"How the Color Question Looks to an American in France"	January 1907
Harper, Frances Ellen Watkins	"The Woman's Christian Temperance Union and the Colored Woman"	January 1888
	"National Woman's Christian Temperance Union"	January 1889
	Symposium on Temperance	April 1891
Howe, Mary W.	Symposium on Temperance	April 1891
Hubert, Lucy	"Women in Society"	October 1903
Jackson, Ida Joyce	"Do Negroes Constitute a Race of Criminals?"	April 1907
Jarvis, Mamie	"Health"	April 1896
Johnson, Lillian	"The Greatest Pictures of the World"	April 1910
Jones, Hannah	"Women as Educators"	April 1893
Joseph, Frances	"Prison Reform Work in New Orleans"	April 1899
Lake, Selena	"Alexander Pope"	January 1895

Lambert, Mary Elizabeth	"A Bunch of Pansies"	October 1884
Lawson, Rosetta	Symposium on Temperance	April 1891
	"The Temperance Reform a World-Wide Movement"	January 1901
Layten, Sarah Willie	"A Northern Phase of a Southern Problem"	April 1910
Lee, Mary Elizabeth Ashe	"The Home-Maker"	July 1891
Mahorney, Gertrude	"Christmas Eve"	October 1899
McDonald, Elizabeth	"Official Service as a Probation Officer in the Cook County Juvenile Court"	January 1904
McKinney, Susan Smith	"Marasmus Infantum"	April 1887
Mossell, Gertrude Bustill	"The Colored Woman in Verse"	July 1885
Mossell, Mary Louisa	"Drummond's 'Greatest Thing in the World'"	April 1892
Noble, Mrs. H. R.	"Fetes for the Czar in Paris"	January 1897
Pemberton, Caroline	"Experiences and Observations in the Black Belt, amid the 'Souls of Black Folk'"	July 1904
Ray, Henrietta Cordelia	"Charles Lamb"	July 1891
Rice, Miss H. A.	"Dr. Sevier"	October 1888
Roberts, Mattie F.	"Which Is the More Useful Art—Painting or Music?"	January 1887
Scarborough, Sarah C	"French Literature of the Thirteenth Century"	July 1885
	"Music in Education"	January 1902
Tanner, Sarah E.	"Henry Wadsworth Longfellow"	October 1895
Taylor, Nora F.	"Echoes from the 12th Episcopal District"	April 1913

Taylor, Mrs. G. E.	"Woman's Work and Influence in Home and Church"	July 1906
Thompson, Lillian Viola	"Beauties in Evangeline"	July 1890
Tillman, Katherine Davis	"Afro-American Women and Their Work"	April 1895
	"The Negro Among Angle Saxon Poets"	July 1897
	"Afro-American Poets and Their Verse"	April 1898
	"Heirs of Slavery: A Little Drama of To-Day"	January 1901
	"Alexandre Dumas, Pére"	January 1907
	"Alexander Sergeivich Pushkin"	July 1909
Turpin, Josephine J.	"The Origin and Progress of the English Language"	January 1885
	"Charles Dickens"	July 1885
	"A Plea for Co-Education of the Sexes"	January 1887
	"A Remedy for War"	October 1887
	"Teaching as a Profession"	October 1888
Washington, Josephine J. Turpin	"The Province of Poetry"	October 1889
	"Lessons in the Life of McKinley"	January 1902
	"What of the Children?"	July 1922
Williams, Fannie Barrier	"The Awakening of Women"	April 1897
	"Suffrage in Illinois"	October 1913
Williams, Sylvanie Francoz	"Action for the Hour"	April 1886
Yates, Josephine Silone (R. K. Potter)	"Natural Science in the Schools"	July 1889
	"Physiology and Hygiene"	April 1890
	"River Systems of the United States," Parts 1 and 2	January 1894, April 1894

	"Municipal Franchises"	April 1895
	"Political Results of the Reformation"	April 1896
	"French Literature in the Seventeenth Century"	January 1901
	"Lincoln the Emancipator"	April 1910
	"Rural Versus Urban"	April 1912

Notes

Introduction

1. All citations to the *A.M.E. Church Review* appear parenthetically in the text.

2. Frances Smith Foster, introduction to Frances Ellen Watkins Harper, *Minnie's Sacrifice, Sowing and Reaping, Trial and Triumph: Three Rediscovered Novels* (Beacon, 1994), xxvi.

3. Frank Luther Mott, *A History of American Magazines, 1740–1930* (Belknap Press of Harvard University Press, 1958), 3:71. For an extended description of the quarterly, see Walter C. Daniel, "*A.M.E. Church Review*," in *Black Journals of the United States* (Greenwood, 1982), 27–32.

4. See "Aunt Lindy" (January 1889), "The Crispus Attucks Monument" (April 1889), "Eugenie's Mistake" (January 1892), and "Zelia: A Story" (July 1892). All appeared under Matthews's pen name, Victoria Earle.

5. Victoria Earle Matthews, "The Value of Race Literature: An Address Delivered at the First Congress of Colored Women of the United States, at Boston, Mass., July 30th, 1895," Yale University Library, https://collections.library.yale.edu/catalog/10171940, 3, 13, 14–15, 21. I am indebted to Brittney C. Cooper's discussion of Matthews's address in *Beyond Respectability: The Intellectual Thought of Race Women* (University of Illinois Press, 2017), 41–42, which points out Matthews's call for these various genres of race literature. The address is reprinted in Shirley Wilson Logan, ed., *With Pen and Voice: A Critical Anthology of Nineteenth-Century African-American Women* (Southern Illinois University Press, 1995). See also Kerstin Rudolph, "Victoria Earle Matthews: Making Literature During the Woman's Era," *Legacy: A Journal of American Women Writers* 33:1 (2016): 103–26, which discusses this address.

6. Terrell also contributed two articles specifically addressing the formation and progress of the National Association of Colored Women: "A Few Possibilities of the National Association of Colored Women" (October 1896), and "The Duty of the National Association of Colored Women to the Race" (January 1900). Terrell's involvement with the association has been discussed both by her biographer, Alison M. Parker, and by Cooper. See Parker, *Unceasing Militant: The Life of Mary Church Terrell* (University of North Carolina Press, 2020); Cooper, *Beyond Respectability*, chap. 2, "'Proper, Dignified Agitation': The Evolution of Mary Church Terrell."

7. Scholars of the Progressive Era identify it as the period between the end of Reconstruction and the close of the First World War, focusing on the decades between 1890 and 1920. It was an era marked by increasing industrialization, the rise of reform movements, and by "sweeping change in every area of politics, society, and culture" (Faith Jaycox, introduction to *The Progressive Era* [Facts on File, 2005], vii). In a January 1888 article for the *Review*, Frances Ellen Watkins Harper quoted Victor Hugo as identifying that moment as "woman's era." Ruffin formed a club in 1893, and *Woman's Era* became the title of the 1894–97 publication resulting from those efforts (Evelyn Brooks Higginbotham, *Righteous Discontent: The Women's Movement in the Black Baptist Church, 1880–1920* [Harvard University Press, 1993], 182). In the introduction to *Post-Bellum, Pre-Harlem: African American Literature and Culture, 1877–1919* (New York University Press, 2006), Barbara McCaskill and Caroline Gebhard note that Charles Chestnutt christened this the postbellum–pre-Harlem period in his collection *Stories, Novels and Essays* (1, 7–8).

8. Higginbotham, *Righteous Discontent*, 6. Digitized copies of *The National Baptist Magazine* are available at the website of the Southern Baptist Historical Library & Archives (accessed August 2, 2025, https://sbhla.org/digital-resources/national-baptist-magazine/).

9. Mia Bay, Farah J. Griffin, Martha S. Jones, and Barbara D. Savage, eds., *Toward an Intellectual History of Black Women* (University of North Carolina Press, 2016); Hettie V. Williams and Melissa Ziobro, eds., *A Seat at the Table: Black Women Public Intellectuals in US History and Culture* (University Press of Mississippi, 2023).

10. Higginbotham's groundbreaking *Righteous Discontent* analyzes the speeches and publications arising from the Woman's Convention, Auxiliary to the National Baptist Convention, and notes the call for a "distinctive literature" (194), but the contributions of Baptist women to denominational publications represent only one of that book's topics. Jualynne E. Dodson explores AME women's efforts to gain power within the denomination in *Engendering Church: Women, Power, and the AME Church* (Rowman & Littlefield, 2002) but does not focus on their contributions to the *A.M.E. Church Review*. Martha S. Jones explores African American women's efforts to gain political rights in *All Bound Up Together: The Woman Question and African American Public Culture, 1830–1900* (University of North Carolina Press, 2007), esp. chap. 5, "Make Us a Power: Churchwomen's

Politics and the Campaign for Women's Rights." Excerpts from a few of the women contributors to the *Review* are included in Stephen W. Angell and Anthony B. Pinn, eds., *Social Protest Thought in the African Methodist Episcopal Church, 1862–1939* (University of Tennessee Press, 2000). However, their study focuses narrowly on "social protest" literature.

11. As of 2025, the Center for Research Libraries has digitized just over a dozen issues from 1892 to 1896. Although dozens of issues are available at the Internet Archive, most are from the mid- to late twentieth century. The Library of Congress has digitized five issues: 1895, 1900, 1912, 1913, and 1914.

12. Joycelyn Moody, *Sentimental Confessions: Spiritual Narratives of Nineteenth-Century African American Women* (University of Georgia Press, 2001), 176.

13. Andreá N. Williams, "Recovering Black Women Writers in Periodical Archives," *American Periodicals* 27:1 (2017): 25–28. See also special issue, "Black Periodical Studies," ed. Eric Gardner and Joycelyn Moody, *American Periodicals* 25:2 (2015); special issue, "African American Print Culture," ed. Joycelyn Moody and Howard Rambsy II, *MELUS* 50:3 (2015).

14. A welcome exception to this situation is found in Gardner's work, especially his meticulous use of census data to flesh out information about readers and contributors to *The Christian Recorder*. His work serves as a model for the biobibliographic material included in this project. See Eric Gardner, *Black Print Unbound: The Christian Recorder, African American Literature, and Periodical Culture* (Oxford University Press, 2015), esp. chap. 5, "'We Are in the World': Reading the *Recorder* in the Civil War Era," and chap. 6, "'So Let Us Hear from All the Brethren': The *Christian Recorder* and Correspondence."

15. I borrow the term *biobibliography* from Eric Gardner, "Children's Literature in the *Christian Recorder*: An Initial Comparative Biobibliography for May 1862 and April 1973," in *Who Writes for Black Children? African American Children's Literature Before 1900*, ed. Katharine Capshaw and Anna Mae Duane (University of Minnesota Press, 2017).

16. Cooper, *Beyond Respectability*, 34–35.

17. Andreá N. Williams, *Dividing Lines: Class Anxiety and Postbellum Black Fiction* (University of Michigan Press, 2012), 4–5, 3.

18. Mia Bay, "The Battle for Womanhood Is the Battle for Race," in *Toward an Intellectual History of Black Women*, ed. Bay et al., 86–87.

19. Penelope Bullock, *The Afro-American Periodical Press, 1838–1909* (Louisiana State University Press, 1981), 39–40, 13, 18, 41.

20. Gardner, *Black Print Unbound*, 11.

21. Bullock, *Afro-American Periodical Press*, 14, 16–17, 18, 44.

22. Daniel, *Black Journals*, 27.

23. David W. Wills, "Aspects of Social Thought in the African Methodist Episcopal Church, 1884–1910" (PhD diss., Harvard University, 1975), 162, 163. Wills's

focus on the first five years of the *Review*'s publication means that the increased contributions of women during the 1890s (particularly under Kealing's editorship) fall outside the scope of his study.

24. I tallied the number of pages in each issue authored by men and the number that could be clearly identified as having been written by women. I excluded the back matter—for example, "Miscellaneous," "Book Reviews," or "Editorials." Where the name was ambiguous regarding gender, I counted that submission as authored by a male writer.

25. Derrick R. Spires, "*Aliened Americans*: Pseudonymity and Gender Politics in Early Black Social Media," *African American Review* 55:1 (2022): 33–49.

26. See Hallie Q. Brown, "Josephine Silone Yates," in *Homespun Heroines and Other Women of Distinction* (Oxford University Press, 1988), 179. See also Gary R. Kremer and Cindy M. Mackey, "The Life and Work of Josephine Silone Yates," *Missouri Historical Review* 90:2 (1986): 201.

27. Cooper, *Beyond Respectability*, 34. See W. E. B. Du Bois, "Two Negro Conventions," *The Independent*, September 7, 1899.

28. Derrick R. Spires, *The Practice of Citizenship: Black Politics and Print Culture in the Early United States* (University of Pennsylvania Press, 2019), 2–3.

29. Bay, "Battle for Womanhood," 76.

30. See Laurie F. Maffly-Kipp and Kathryn Lofton, eds., *Women's Work: An Anthology of African-American Women's Historical Writings from Antebellum America to the Harlem Renaissance* (Oxford University Press, 2010).

31. Andreá N. Williams, *Dividing Lines*, 3.

32. See, for example, Stephen Turner, "Who's Afraid of the History of Sociology?" *Swiss Journal of Sociology* 24:1 (1998): 3–10. See also Anthony J. Blasi, ed., *Diverse Histories of American Sociology* (Brill, 2005), which points out that the History of Sociology Section of the American Sociological Association was not formed until 1999 and that many sociologists actively resisted the historicization of the field's development.

33. Patricia Hill Collins, *Black Feminist Thought: Knowledge, Consciousness, and the Politics of Empowerment*, 2nd ed. (Routledge, 2009), 33; Delores P. Aldridge, *Imagine a World: Pioneering Black Women Sociologists* (University Press of America, 2009), xiii.

34. See Elizabeth McHenry, *Forgotten Readers: Recovering the Lost History of African American Literary Societies* (Duke University Press, 2002); Audrey Thomas McCluskey, *A Forgotten Sisterhood: Pioneering Black Women Educators and Activists in the Jim Crow South* (Rowman & Littlefield, 2014); Gholdy Muhammad, *Cultivating Genius: An Equity Framework for Culturally and Historically Responsive Literacy* (Scholastic, 2020); Crystal Lynn Webster, *Beyond the Boundaries of Childhood: African American Children in the Antebellum North* (University of North Carolina Press, 2021); Heather Andrea Williams, *Self-Taught:*

African American Education in Slavery and Freedom (University of North Carolina Press, 2007).

35. Xine Yao, *Disaffected: The Cultural Politics of Unfeeling in Nineteenth-Century America* (Duke University Press, 2021), 146; Ruth J. Abram, ed., *"Send Us a Lady Physician": Women Doctors in America, 1835–1920* (Norton, 1985), 57.

36. Yao, *Disaffected*, 138.

Chapter 1: Beyond "Creation and Transmission of Literary Culture"

1. Wills, "Aspects of Social Thought," 163.
2. Moody, *Sentimental Confessions*, 17–18.
3. For more on Washington's life, see Rita B. Dandridge, introduction to *The Collected Essays of Josephine J. Turpin Washington: A Black Reformer in the Post-Reconstruction South*, edited by Rita B. Dandridge (Charlottesville: University of Virginia Press, 2019), xi–xxxii; I. Garland Penn, *The Afro-American Press and Its Editors* (Wiley, 1891), 393–96.
4. W. S. Scarborough, *The Autobiography of William Sanders Scarborough: An American Journey from Slavery to Scholarship*, ed. Michele Valerie Ronnick (Wayne State University Press, 2005), 34; finding aid, W. S. Scarborough Scrapbook, Manuscript Collection 1021, Stuart A. Rose Manuscript, Archives, and Rare Book Library, Emory University, Atlanta, accessed November 18, 2019, https://archives.libraries.emory.edu/repositories/7/resources/3350; Elizabeth Renker, "'American Literature' in the College Curriculum: Three Case Studies, 1890–1910," *ELH* 67:3 (2000): 858. For one of several scholars who assumed that Sarah Scarborough was African American, see Paula Giddings, *In Search of Sisterhood: Delta Sigma Theta and the Challenge of the Black Sorority Movement* (Perennial, 2002), 68, which asserts that Sarah Scarborough was a founding member of the sorority's Wilberforce chapter and that the Scarborough home was often referred to as the Delta House. Michele Valerie Ronnick, correspondence with author, July 20, 2021. For more on William Sanders Scarborough, see Scarborough, *Autobiography*. Ronnick's dogged research has provided a more complete picture of Sarah Scarborough's life and work, which is the subject of Ronnick's forthcoming book.
5. AME historian Dennis C. Dickerson notes that the 1870s and 1880s saw the expansion of the denomination's evangelism racially and ethnically. The Exoduster movement of the 1880s encouraged Black migration to the Kansas and Nebraska Territories and expanded the possibilities for evangelizing in Indian Territory. In addition, the church called for an effort to reach out to the Chinese in California (*The African Methodist Episcopal Church: A History* [Cambridge University Press, 2020], 150–51).

6. Dandridge, introduction, xxii. This volume includes "The Province of Poetry."
7. Dandridge, introduction, xxiv–xxv.
8. Shirley Samuels, ed., *The Culture of Sentiment: Race, Gender, and Sentimentality in Nineteenth-Century America* (Oxford University Press, 1992), 3; P. Gabrielle Foreman, *Activist Sentiments: Reading Black Women in the Nineteenth-Century* (University of Illinois Press, 2009), 3. The fifteen essays in Samuels's volume treat poetry, fiction, artwork, and other cultural forms. Foreman's study focuses primarily on the fiction of Harriet Jacobs, Harriet E. Wilson, Frances Ellen Watkins Harper, Emma Dunham Kelley-Hawkins, and Amelia E. Johnson.
9. The attribution appears in Dandridge, introduction, xviii.
10. The first three installments were "Part I: "French Literature in the Twelfth and Thirteenth Centuries" (October 1897, 219–27); "Part II: French Literature in the Fourteenth and Fifteenth Centuries" (January 1898, 306–17); "Part III: French Literature in the Sixteenth Century—Period of the Renaissance" (July 1899, 113–23).
11. Daniel Hack, *Reaping Something New: African American Transformations of Victorian Literature* (Princeton University Press, 2017), 2.
12. See the following essays contributed by male writers: J. W. Manning, "Shakespeare's Iago" (July 1889); A. Arnold Morin, "Hamlet: A Study in Mental Physiology" (April 1890); A. Arnold Morin, "John Bunyan and His Times" (January 1891); A. Arnold Morin, "Biographical Sketch of Condorcet" (April 1891); Lewis B. Moore, "A Study of Homer" (October 1893); T. McCants Stewart, "Whittier: Poet of Freedom" (January 1894); Everett J. Waring, "The Shakespearean School of Ethics" (January 1895) (a reprint of a March 23, 1894, lecture delivered at the YMCA of Washington, DC); H. T. Kealing, "Tolstoy as a Force in Religion" (January 1911); H. T. Kealing, "The Interpretation of Poe's Raven" (April 1912).
13. See the biography of Ray in Jessie Carney Smith, ed., *Notable Black American Women* (Gale, 1992–96), 1:924–25; Hallie Q. Brown, "Henrietta Cordelia Ray," in *Homespun Heroines*, 172.
14. Hallie Q. Brown, "Sarah Elizabeth Tanner," in *Homespun Heroines*, 32.
15. Brown, "Sarah Elizabeth Tanner," 33.
16. This is likely the same Selena C. Lake who in December 1888 was a student at the Colored School 1 in New York City. According to the *Brooklyn (New York) Daily Eagle*, December 15, 1888, Lake read a poem, "Gradation," at a ceremony.
17. Frazelia Campbell, Find a Grave, accessed July 26, 2025, https://www.findagrave.com/memorial/83162444/frazelia-campbell; Fanny Jackson Coppin, *Reminiscences of School Life and Hints on Teaching* (1913; Hall, 1995), 154; Frazelia Campbell, 1880 US Census, Philadelphia, Pennsylvania, roll 1170, p. 275c, ED 134; "Campbell, Frazelia," *Rutgers Database of Classical Scholars*, accessed December 6, 2019, https://dbcs.rutgers.edu/all-scholars/8590-campbell-frazelia. For the same

photograph of Campbell, see Michele Valerie Ronnick, "Early African-American Scholars in the Classics: A Photographic Essay," *Journal of Blacks in Higher Education* 43 (2004): 101–5.

18. "School No. 67," *Brooklyn (New York) Citizen*, June 29, 1889.

19. T. W. Henderson, *The Doctrine and Discipline of the African Methodist Episcopal Church*, 21st rev. ed. (AME Book Concern, 1896), contains numerous references to matrimony, one of the five sacraments (2). In addition, "Matrimonial Regulations" 81–82) established guidelines for choosing a mate, while "Solemnization of Matrimony" (224–32) provided language for publishing the banns and conducting the marriage ceremony.

20. Mary L. Tanner, 1870 US Census, Frederick Ward 2, Frederick, Maryland, roll M593_586, p. 62B; Mary Louisa Tanner, *Philadelphia, Pennsylvania, Marriage Index, 1885–1951* (database online), accessed December 6, 2019, Ancestry.com; John Clay Smith, *Emancipation: The Making of the Black Lawyer, 1844–1944* (University Press of Pennsylvania, 1993), 153.

21. Henderson, *Doctrine and Discipline*, 328.

22. See Steven R. Barnett, "Gertrude Amelia Mahorney," 2018, Indiana Commission for Women: Writing Her Story, https://www.in.gov/icw/files/20180305-Mahorney,-Gertrude-Amelia.pdf.

23. Eligio Martinez Jr., "Virginia State University (1882–)," BlackPast, January 10, 1810, https://www.blackpast.org/african-american-history/virginia-state-university-1882/; *Richmond (Virginia) Planet*, June 12, 1886; "The Labor of Twenty-Five Years," *Charlotte (North Carolina) Daily Observer*, November 22, 1908; M. A. Majors, "Lucinda Bragg Adams," in *Noted Negro Women: Their Triumphs and Activities* (Donohue & Henneberry, 1893), 215.

24. The 1910 census lists Andrew N. Johnson, age forty-three, as an undertaker and Lillian Johnson as a bookkeeper, likely for her husband's business. See 1910 US Census, Nashville Ward 6, Davidson, Tennessee, roll T624_1495, p. 1a, ED 0030.

25. 1910 US Census, Nashville Ward 6, Davidson, Tennessee, roll T624_1495, p. 1a, ED 0030; editorial, *A.M.E. Church Review*, January 1909. "Society News," *Nashville (Tennessee) Globe*, April 20, 1917.

Chapter 2: AME Churchwomen Making History

1. Maffly-Kipp and Lofton, *Women's Work*, 4.

2. Maffly-Kipp and Lofton, *Women's Work*, 8. See also Bay et al., *Toward an Intellectual History of Black Women*, as well as the groundbreaking work of Frances Smith Foster, particularly *Written by Herself: Literary Production by African American Women, 1746–1892* (Indiana University Press, 1993).

3. I am indebted to Andreá N. Williams for suggesting the term *intellectual cosmopolitanism* and for suggesting that I consider the ways in which this work sought to position Black Americans in relation to other oppressed peoples around the world.

4. For an excellent discussion of the various representations of Crispus Attucks, see Mitch Kachun, *First Martyr of Liberty: Crispus Attucks in American Memory* (Oxford University Press, 2017).

5. Brown, "Josephine Silone Yates," 179; Kremer and Mackey, "Life and Work of Josephine Silone Yates," 201, 204, 200, 208.

6. Penn, *Afro-American Press*, 393–96. See also Josephine J. Turpin Washington, *Collected Essays*, which includes but does not discuss this essay.

7. Maffly-Kipp and Lofton, *Women's Work*, 3.

8. Cooper, *Beyond Respectability*, 26–27.

9. Gertrude Bustill Mossell, "The Afro-American Woman in Verse," in *The Work of the Afro-American Woman* (Ferguson, 1894), 67–97.

10. See Katherine Davis Chapman Tillman, *The Works of Katherine Davis Chapman Tillman*, ed. Claudia Tate (Oxford University Press, 1991). Although this volume includes these essays, Tate offers very little discussion of them and instead focuses on Tillman's short and serial fiction, drama, and poetry.

11. Claudia Tate, introduction to *Works of Katherine Davis Chapman Tillman*, 11; Maffly-Kipp and Lofton, *Women's Work*, 150; 1910 US Census, Pasadena Ward 2, Los Angeles, roll T624-86, p. 8b, ED 0305; "A Noted Woman Dies," *Kansas City (Kansas) Advocate*, December 7, 1923. Tillman's poem "The Pastor" was dedicated to her husband. She read "an original poem on Bishop William Paul Quinn" at the a 1915 meeting of the AME churches held in Hannibal, Missouri ("Hospital Dedicated; Ready for Occupancy," *Chicago Defender*, July 17, 1905). She also delivered a 1914 lecture, "The Ideal Negro Woman," at Chicago's St. Mary's AME Church (*Chicago Defender*, August 8, 1914). Tate's pioneering work in the 1980s made much of Tillman's writing readily available, but limitations on the availability of sources at the time restricted the biographical data that could be found.

12. Rodger Streitmatter, *Raising Her Voice: African-American Women Journalists Who Changed History* (University Press of Kentucky, 1994), 37–48.

13. For more on Black women's scrapbooking, see Ellen Gruber Garvey, *Writing with Scissors: American Scrapbooks from the Civil War to the Harlem Renaissance* (Oxford University Press, 2013), esp. chap. 4, "Alternative Histories in African American Scrapbooks."

14. Mossell, "Afro-American Woman in Verse," 80–81, 82, 78.

15. See Hallie Q. Brown, *Pen Pictures of Pioneers of Wilberforce* (Aldine, 1937), 49–51.

16. For an extended biographical sketch of Laney, see Audrey Thomas McCluskey, "Building Character and Culture: Lucy Craft Laney and the Haines

School Community," in *African American Women Educators: A Critical Examination of Their Pedagogies, Educational Ideas, and Activism from the Nineteenth to the Mid-Twentieth Century*, ed. Karen A. Johnson, Abul Pitre, and Kenneth L. Johnson (Rowman & Littlefield, 2014).

17. AME churchwomen received greater recognition with R. R. Wright, comp., *The Encyclopaedia of the African Methodist Episcopal Church*, 2nd ed. (Book Concern of the AME Church, 1947).

18. For more on advice columns for Black women, see Nazera Sadiq Wright, *Black Girlhood in the Nineteenth Century* (University of Illinois Press, 2016), esp. chap. 3, "'Teach Your Daughters': Black Girlhood and Mrs. N. F. Mossell's Advice Column in the *New York Freeman*."

19. Tate, introduction, 10–11.

20. I have been unable to find this editorial.

21. In October 1899 issue of the *Review*, Kealing notes that the "old school Christian" objects to the reading of any kind of fiction and that novel reading, card playing, and dancing are generally to be eschewed. However, he also points out that both novels and drama have religious origins and that wise teachers can assign carefully chosen novels (278–81).

22. See Kimberlé Williams Crenshaw, "Demarginalizing the Intersection of Race and Sex: A Black Feminist Critique of Antidiscrimination Doctrine, Feminist Theory and Antiracist Politics," *University of Chicago Legal Forum* 140 (1989): 139–67.

Chapter 3: Sociological Writings: Home, Family, Church

1. Stephen Turner, *American Sociology: From Pre-Disciplinary to Post-Normal* (Palgrave Macmillan, 2014), 6–7, 9.

2. See Lynn McDonald, *The Women Founders of the Social Sciences* (McGill-Queens University Press, 1994).

3. Mary Jo Deegan, ed., *Women in Sociology: A Bio-Bibliographical Sourcebook* (Greenwood, 1991), 15; Mary Jo Deegan, "Early Women Sociologists and the American Sociological Society: The Patterns of Exclusion and Participation," *American Sociologist* 16:1 (1981): 14–24; Mary Jo Deegan, "W. E. B. Du Bois and the Women of Hull-House, 1895–1899," *American Sociologist* 19:4 (1988): 301–11. The focus on the home, women, children, and the family remains a key part of the American Sociological Association's definition of the field: "Sociology is the study of social life, social change, and the social causes and consequences of human behavior. Sociologists investigate the structure of groups, organizations, and societies and how people interact within these contexts. Since all human behavior is social, the subject matter of sociology ranges from the intimate family to global communities; from deviance to organized crime; from religious traditions to state

institutions; and from the divisions of race, gender and social class to the shared beliefs of a common culture" ("What Is Sociology?" American Sociological Association, March 14, 2024, https://www.asanet.org/about/what-is-sociology).

4. Collins, *Black Feminist Thought*, 33; Aldridge, *Imagine a World*, xiii.

5. Mary Jo Deegan, "Editor's Preface," in *The New Woman of Color: The Collected Writings of Fannie Barrier Williams, 1893–1918*, ed. Mary Jo Deegan (Northern Illinois University Press, 2002). See also Wanda A. Hendricks, *Fannie Barrier Williams: Crossing the Borders of Region and Race* (University of Illinois Press, 2014).

6. See Mary Jo Deegan, "Transcending a Patriarchal and Racist Past: African American Women in Sociology, 1890–1920," *Sociological Origins* 2:1 (2000): 37–54; Deegan, "Early Woman Sociologists and the American Sociological Society"; Deegan, "W. E. B. Du Bois and the Women of Hull-House"; Lee Hedwig and Christina Hughes, "#SayHerName: Why Black Women Matter in Sociology," in *The New Black Sociologists: Historical and Contemporary Perspectives*, ed. Marcus A. Hunter (Routledge, 2018); Morris, *Scholar Denied*. See also W. E. B. Du Bois, *W. E. B. Du Bois on Sociology and the Black Community*, ed. Dan S. Green and Edwin D. Driver (University of Chicago Press, 1978); Elmer P. Martin and Joanne M. Martin, *Spirituality and the Black Helping Tradition in Social Work* (NASW Press, 2002).

7. Deegan, *Women in Sociology*, 7. The appendix offers a list of sixty-four additional women whom Deegan considers early sociologists.

8. William Seraile, *Fire in His Heart: Bishop Benjamin Tucker Tanner and the A.M.E. Church* (University of Tennessee Press, 1998), 52, 103, 47, 48, 124–25.

9. Shelley P. Haley, introduction to Coppin, *Fanny Jackson Coppin*, xxxii, xxx; Bullock, *Afro-American Periodical Press*, 94.

10. See Barbara Welter, "The Cult of True Womanhood: 1820–1860," *American Quarterly* 18:2 (1966): 151–74. On the AME denomination's attitudes regarding women's roles, see Julius H. Bailey, *Around the Family Altar: Domesticity in the African Methodist Episcopal Church, 1865–1890* (University Press of Florida, 2005).

11. *Merriam-Webster Dictionary Online*, "didactic," accessed September 15, 2024, https://www.merriam-webster.com/dictionary/didactic.

12. Collins, *Black Feminist Thought*, 33; Aldridge, *Imagining a World*, xiii.

13. Seraile, *Fire in His Heart*, 5.

14. G. E. Taylor is likely Green Taylor, who served four years as editor of *The Southern Christian Recorder* and died on December 9, 1908, of a "painful illness" and "incurable affection" [sic] (Mrs. G. E. Taylor, "The Death of Dr. G. E. Taylor," *A.M.E. Church Review*, January 1909). The author of "Woman's Work and Influence in Home and Church" was not Taylor's first wife, who died in April 1900, while he was attending the Texas General Conference ("The Following Sad Lines Come from Dr. G. E. Taylor of Texas," *Christian Recorder*, April 5, 1900).

15. Given the author's preoccupation with marital infidelity, the death of Taylor's first wife, and the causes given for Taylor's death, it is possible that Taylor had

a sexually transmitted disease. Such ailments constituted a real concern in this era but often appear as coded references in the popular literature of the day such as Charlotte Perkins Gilman's *The Crux*.

16. For more on the Women's Parent Mite Missionary Society and its later rival, the Women's Home and Foreign Missionary Society, organized by Bishop Henry McNeal Turner in the southern states in 1896, see Bettye Collier-Thomas, *Jesus, Jobs, and Justice: African American Women and Religion* (Knopf, 2010), 151–68.

17. Richard Robert Wright Jr., *Who's Who in the General Conference, 1924* (AME Book Concern, 1924), 11; A. E. Perts, "A Happy Marriage," *Christian Recorder*, May 10, 1900. On Chappelle's service to the Women's Home and Foreign Missionary Society, see L. L. Berry, *A Century of Missions of the African Methodist Episcopal Church, 1840–1940* (Gutenberg, 1942), 250.

18. Richard R. Wright Jr., "Chappelle, William David," in *The Centennial Encyclopaedia of the African Methodist Episcopal Church* (Book Concern of the AME Church, 1916), 65.

19. For AME deaconesses and women evangelists, see Jualynne Dodson, "Nineteenth-Century A.M.E. Preaching Women: Cutting Edge of Women's Inclusion in Church Polity," in *Women in New Worlds: Historical Perspectives on the Wesleyan Tradition*, ed. Hilah F. Thomas and Rosemary Skinner Keller (Abingdon, 1981).

CHAPTER 4: SOCIOLOGICAL WRITINGS: SUFFRAGE, TEMPERANCE, CRIMINALITY, PRISON REFORM

1. Brigitte Fielder and Jonathan Senchyne, eds., *Against a Sharp White Background: Infrastructures of African American Print* (University of Wisconsin Press, 2019), 6.

2. Hendricks, *Fannie Barrier Williams*, ix. Williams may have been "elite," but Mary Jo Deegan disputes earlier scholars' labeling of Williams as "elitist," as an "accommodationist," or as a "dilettante" (introduction to Williams, *New Woman of Color*, xv).

3. Cooper, *Beyond Respectability*, 38.

4. Hendricks, *Fannie Barrier Williams*, ix.

5. Deegan, introduction, xiii–lx.

6. "Among the Churches," *Gazette* (York, Pennsylvania), February 14, 1901; "Women's Day at Siloam," *Delaware County Daily Times* (Carlisle, Pennsylvania), November 22, 1902; Lucy E. Hubert, *Hints on the Care of Children* (Ferguson, 1898). I discovered this volume while completing a residential research fellowship at the Library Company of Philadelphia. As far as I can determine, no scholarship yet exists on book-length Black women's advice literature. On conduct literature targeting Black children, see Nazera Sadiz Wright, "'Our Hope Is in the Rising

Generation'": Locating African American Children's Literature in the Children's Department of *The Colored American*," in *Who Writes for Black Children?* ed. Capshaw and Duane. Although this book does not specifically treat "conduct literature" published in the *Review*, women did contribute original articles in this genre. See, for example, Frances Ellen Watkins Harper, "True and False Politeness" (January 1898, 339–45).

7. [3] *Xenia [Ohio] Daily Gazette*, January 4, 1890, September 30, 1903; *St. Louis Globe-Democrat*, August 13, 1904. For the formation of the National Grand Chapter of the Order of Eastern Star, see *Washington (DC) Bee*, August 23, 1902. Dickinson presented a paper, "The Order of the Eastern Star," at the 1904 national convention of the Colored Scottish Rite Masons in St. Louis (*St. Louis Globe-Democrat*, August 13, 1904). For Dickerson's travels across the United States, see *Xenia (Ohio) Daily Gazette*, July 6, 1903, January 7, 1907.

8. Stephen W. Angell and Anthony B. Pinn, "The A.M.E. Church on the Social Gospel and Socialism," in *Social Protest Thought*, ed. Angell and Pinn.

9. Effie B. Carter, 1910 US Census, Xenia, Greene, Ohio, roll T624_1185, p. 14a, ED 0099; R. R. Wright, *Encyclopaedia of the African Methodist Episcopal Church*, 435. For the commencement, see *New York Age*, July 7, 1910. Information accessed on Ancestry.com, October 21, 2019.

10. Philip S. Foner, "Caroline Hollingsworth Pemberton: Philadelphia Socialist Champion of Black Equality," *Pennsylvania History: A Journal of Mid-Atlantic Studies* 43:3 (1976): 226–51. See also John David Smith, *An Old Creed for the New South: Proslavery Ideology and Historiography, 1865–1918* (Southern Illinois University Press, 2008), esp. chap. 3, "Antislavery Thought from Reconstruction to Reconciliation." See Caroline E.[sic] Pemberton, "The Poor and Those Whom They Make Rich," *Selma Morning Times*, March 7, 1904, which describes her as a "Sociologist, of Philadelphia." Pemberton's article was reprinted in the *Springville (New York) Journal*, March 17, 1904, and in the *Leon (Iowa) Journal-Reporter*, March 31, 1904.

11. Aldon D. Morris, *The Scholar Denied: W. E. B. Du Bois and the Birth of Modern Sociology* (University of California Press, 2015).

12. Hallie Q. Brown, "Madame Emma Azalia Hackley," in *Homespun Heroines*; Benjamin Griffith Brawley, *The Negro in Literature and Art in the United States* (Duffield, 1918), 140.

13. Leonora Beck Ellis, "The Southern Negro as a Property-Owner," *Tom Watson's Magazine*, June 1905, 428–34. The *Review* erroneously gave the author's first name as *Leona*. See also Thomas E. Watson, "Editorials—Our Creed," *Tom Watson's Magazine*, June 1905, 385.

14. Leonora Beck Ellis, "A Study of Southern Cotton-Mill Communities: Child Labor; The Operatives in General," *American Journal of Sociology* 8:5 (1903): 623–30. Notice of this publication appeared in *Atlanta Constitution*, April 2, 1903; Linda

Grant, Marybeth C. Stalp, and Kathryn B. Ward, "Women's Sociological Research and Writing in the *AJS* in the Pre–World War II Era," *American Sociologist* 33:3 (2002): 69–91. See also Mary Jo Deegan, "Transcending a Patriarchal Past: Teaching the History of Women in Sociology" *Teaching Sociology* 16:2 (1988): 141–50.

15. Collier-Thomas, *Jesus, Jobs and Justice*, 127–30; "Women of NBC Hear Address by Mrs. Layten," *Chicago Tribune*, September 18, 1943. See also Higginbotham, *Righteous Discontent*, 157–58. Scholars of women's early contributions to sociology seem to have missed Layten's addresses and writings on sociology and social reform: for example, Deegan's significant body of scholarship contains no references to Layten.

16. For more on Kellor, see Deegan, *Women in Sociology*, 209–16.

17. See J. W. Hood, "A Bible View of the Evil of Intemperance," (July 1885); A. A. Burleigh, "Prohibition and the Race Problem" (January 1887); J. P. Sampson, "The Prohibition Party" (July 1887); I. S. Tuppins, "Alcohol, Its Use and the Results of Abuse" (July 1888); J. O. Peterson, "A Temperance Talk" (January 1890); D. B. Williams, "The Evil Effects of Intemperance in the Use of Alcoholic Drinks" (April 1890); John W. Norris, "Temperance in the Public Schools and in the Sunday-Schools Equally Essential" (July 1893); J. Goins, "Temperance" (April 1894); E. Johnson, "Temperance" (October 1917).

18. See, for example, "Prohibition in Pennsylvania" (Editorial, July 1889); "The Growth of Prohibition Sentiment" (Sociological, July 1903); "Temperance Experiment," (Religious, July 1906); "A Family of Temperance Workers" (Women, July 1907); "The Growing Temperance Tide" (Editorial, January 1908); "Temperance" (Religious, April 1908); "National Prohibition" (Within the Sphere of Letters, October 1918); "The Ratification of the Federal Prohibition Amendment" (Editorial, April 1919).

19. Foster, introduction to Harper, *Minnie's Sacrifice*, xv; William Carroll, "Frances Ellen Watkins Harper," EBSCO Research Starters, 2023, https://www.ebsco.com/research-starters/history/frances-ellen-watkins-harper. See also Frances Smith Foster, introduction to Frances Ellen Watkins Harper, *A Brighter Coming Day: A Frances Ellen Watkins Harper Reader* (Feminist Press of the City University of New York, 1990). For Harper's children's stories, see Gardner, "Children's Literature in the *Christian Recorder*." See also Marcia Robinson and Milton C. Sernett, "Frances Ellen Watkins Harper," National Abolition Hall of Fame and Museum, accessed September 10, 2024, https://www.nationalabolitionhalloffameandmuseum.org/frances-watkins-harper.html.

20. "The Woman's Christian Temperance Union and the Colored Woman" is reprinted in Harper, *Brighter Coming Day*, 281–84. See also Ruth Bordin, "'A Baptism of Power and Liberty'": The Woman's Crusade of 1873–1874," *Ohio History Journal* 87:4 (1978): 393–404.

21. *Daily Review* (Wilmington, North Carolina), October 5, 1887; *Christian Recorder*, February 21, 1891. In 1899, firefighters were called to put out a blaze

at the home of "a colored woman, Mary W. Howe, No. 612 South Fourth Street" (*Wilmington Messenger*, May 3, 1899). W. T. Anderson was one of the 1887 founders of Campbell College, which was originally located in Vicksburg, Mississippi, but later moved to Jackson. The same man may be the "Rev. W. T. Anderson" who served St. John AME Church in Cleveland, Ohio, in 1896–97; the 1898 Cleveland telephone directory lists "Rev. William T. Anderson" as that congregation's minister. Anderson also served as a chaplain in Cuba during the Spanish-American War (*Cleveland Plain Dealer*, August 19, 1897). Anderson was listed as an 1881 and 1883 graduate of Wilberforce University. See R. R. Wright, *Encyclopaedia of the African Methodist Episcopal Church*, 344, 357, 457. Campbell College closed in 1964 after many years of financial duress (Thomas John Carey, "Campbell College," *Mississippi Encyclopedia*," accessed October 25, 2019, http://mississippiencyclopedia.org/entries/campbell-college).

22. Bay, "Battle for Womanhood," 81.

23. "Rosetta E. Coakley Lawson," in *Notable Black American Women* (Gale, 1996), accessed October 25, 2019.

24. Chanta M. Haywood, *Prophesying Daughters: Black Women Preachers and the Word, 1823–1913* (University of Missouri Press, 2003), 10; "Louisiana Conference," *Christian Recorder*, April 5, 1900; "Mrs. Frances Joseph," *Christian Recorder*, June 14, 1900; "To Better Race, Plan to Establish a Training School for Young Negroes," *Times Democrat* (New Orleans), February 27, 1902. Haywood devotes a portion of chapter 6 to a discussion of Frances Joseph Gaudet's autobiography, *He Leadeth Me* (Louisiana Printing, 1913), but does not examine her published periodical writings. The *Times-Democrat* closely followed the school's progress, featuring a lengthy article with three photographs of the children and the school on December 13, 1909, and noting the groundbreaking for a new girls' dormitory on November 24, 1910.

25. Haywood, *Prophesying Daughters*, 95.

26. D. D. Buck, *The Progression of the Race in the United States and Canada* (Atwell, 1907), 321.

27. "Funds for Mrs. Curtis," *Inter-Ocean* (Chicago), October 2, 1899; Elizabeth McDonald, 1910 US Census, Chicago Ward 31, Cook, Illinois, roll T624_277, p. 21a, ED 1356; Ida D. Lewis, "West Side Woman's Club," *Chicago Defender*, October 8, 1910; "Converted in Convict's Cell," *Chicago Tribune*, March 24, 1903. For publishing information on *The Broad Ax*, see James P. Danky and Maureen E. Hady, eds., *African-American Newspapers and Periodicals: A National Bibliography* (Harvard University Press, 1998), 116. McDonald's photograph appeared in *The Broad Ax* between October 10, 1903, and December 28, 1907.

28. *Broad Ax* (Chicago), September 9, 1916; "Meeting of the Directors of the Louise Training School for Colored Boys," *Broad Ax* (Salt Lake City), September 8, 1917; *Broad Ax* (Salt Lake City), August 23, 1919; Anne Meis Knupfer,

"African-American Facilities for Dependent and Delinquent Children in Chicago, 1900 to 1920: The Louise Juvenile School and the Amanda Smith School," *Journal of Sociology and Social Welfare* 24:3 (1997): 202.

29. Frank Lincoln Mather, *Who's Who of the Colored Race* (Mather, 1915), 150; Barksdale Hamlett, *History of Education in Kentucky* (Kentucky Department of Education, 1914), 288; "Purity of the Home," *Topeka (Kansas) Plaindealer*, August 21, 1903; "Says Future of Race Rests with Its Mothers," *St. Louis Republic*, July 15, 1904; Carrie W. Clifford, "Of Interest to Women," *Alexander's Magazine*, July 15, 1905, 40.

30. "Leader of Colored Women Appeals for Square Deal!" *Topeka Plaindealer*, March 1, 1907.

Chapter 5: E. Marie Carter's "Notes of Travel" Column, 1903-1912

1. Peter Farrelly, dir., *Green Book* (Universal Pictures, 2018); Candacy Taylor, *Overground Railroad: The Green Book and the Roots of Black Travel in America* (Abrams, 2020). On Taylor's *Green Book* project, see Candacy Taylor website, accessed September 10, 2019, http://www.taylormadeculture.com.

2. Bay et al., *Toward an Intellectual History of Black Women*; Foster, *Written by Herself*. See also Farah J. Griffin and Cheryl J. Fish, eds., *A Stranger in the Village: Two Centuries of African-American Travel Writing* (Beacon, 1998); Cheryl J. Fish, *Black and White Women's Travel Narratives: Antebellum Explorations* (University Press of Florida, 2004); Carla L. Peterson, *"Doers of the Word": African American Women Speakers and Writers of the North, 1830–1880* (Oxford University Press, 1995), esp. chap. 3, "Humble Instruments in the Hands of God": Maria Stewart, Jarena Lee, and the Economy of Spiritual Narrative," and chap. 4, "Colored Tourists": Nancy Prince, Mary Ann Shadd Cary, Ethnographic Writing, and the Question of Home."

3. Wills, "Aspects of Social Thought," 175.

4. I began using the term *feminized sociology* in the early stages of the research and writing of this book, years before I discovered Stephen Turner's use of the phrase in his history-of-sociology work, including *American Sociology*, 3.

5. See esp. Psyche Williams-Forson, "Where Did They Eat? Where Did They Stay: Interpreting the Material Culture of Black Women's Domesticity in the Context of the Colored Conventions," in *The Colored Convention Movement: Black Organizing in the Nineteenth Century*, ed. P. Gabrielle Foreman, Jim Casey, and Sarah Lynn Patterson (University of North Carolina Press, 2021), 86–104. For the Colored Conventions Project, see coloredconventions.org, accessed August 21, 2025.

6. Victor H. Green, *The Negro-Motorist Green-Book* (1936; Green, 1940); Taylor website.

7. Mirriam Taggert, *Riding Jane Crow: African American Women on the American Railroad* (University of Illinois Press, 2022), 3, 11; Eric Gardner, "Frances Ellen Watkins Harper's 'National Salvation': A Rediscovered Lecture on Reconstruction." *Common-place* 17:4 (2017): http://common-place.org/book/vol-17-no-4-gardner/; Eric Gardner, "Frances Ellen Watkins Harper's Civil War and Militant Intersectionality," *Mississippi Quarterly* 70–71:4 (2018): 505–18.

8. August Meier and Elliott Rudwick, "The Boycott Movement Against Jim Crow Streetcars in the South, 1900–1906," *Journal of American History* 55:4 (1969): 756–75; Blair L. M. Kelley, *Right to Ride: Streetcar Boycotts and African American Citizenship in the Era of Plessy v. Ferguson* (University of North Carolina Press, 2010). Carter visited Montgomery and Mobile, Alabama; Little Rock, Arkansas; Jacksonville and Pensacola, Florida; Atlanta and Savannah, Georgia; New Orleans and Shreveport, Louisiana: Vicksburg and Natchez, Mississippi; Columbia, South Carolina; Memphis, Nashville, Chattanooga, and Knoxville, Tennessee; San Antonio, Texas; and Richmond, Danville, Portsmouth, Newport News, and Norfolk, Virginia.

9. W. E. B. Du Bois, "Of the Black Belt," in *The Souls of Black Folk* (1903; Library of America, 1986).

10. Karla Slocum, *Black Towns, Black Futures: The Enduring Allure of a Black Place in the American West* (University of North Carolina Press, 2019), 26.

11. Bullock, *Afro-American Periodical Press*, 40–41, 44. For more travel writing by a an African American man, see Mitch Kachun, "The Travels of Col. J. O. Midnight in the New Negro Era: Movement and Constructed Personae in the Activism of Journalist Charles Stewart," paper presented at the African American Intellectual History Society Annual Meeting, Brandeis University, March 30–31, 2018.

12. Eric Gardner, "'Yours for the Cause': The *Christian Recorder* Writings of Lizzie Hart," *Legacy* 27:2 (2010): 367–91.

13. Mia Bay, *To Tell the Truth Freely: The Life of Ida B. Wells* (Hill and Wang, 2009), 62.

14. *A.M.E. Church Review*, April 1904, 382, October 1910, 206; "Miss E. Marie Carter," *Missionary Searchlight*, January 15, 1900; Moses Sheridan, Find a Grave, accessed August 21, 2025, https://www.findagrave.com/memorial/202844733/moses-sheridan; "Illinois Methodists," *St. Louis Palladium*, October 24, 1903; "Commencement," *Christian Recorder*, June 7, 1900; John A. Jackson, *History of Education: from the Greeks to the Present Time*, 2nd ed. (Western Newspaper Union, 1905), 303–4; *Daily News* (Canonsburg, Pennsylvania), September 3, 1904. Her April 1904 column also reports on her stay at Kealing's home, where she received a very warm welcome and "could not help but shed tears, for Creoles believe when much is made over them, they will die soon" (382). A year later, she notes that "the majority of the members of the African Methodist Episcopal Church in the State of Louisiana are of Creole descent" and that the "very best members . . . in New Orleans were once Catholics" (April 1905, 374). According to the title page of *History of Education*,

John Jackson was the former president of the Kentucky Normal and Industrial Institute and of the Lincoln Institute in Jefferson City, Missouri. He was the husband of Ida Joyce Jackson.

15. *Chicago Defender*, January 14, 1928. According to this newspaper report, the couple had been found dead in their St. Louis home on December 31, 1927, with a full dinner on the table. They had last been seen alive on December 24. However, the coroner found no evidence of disease or poison.

16. Founded in 1896 by an act of the General Conference meeting in Wilmington, North Carolina, the Allen Christian Endeavor League was modeled on the worldwide Christian Endeavor movement and designed to engage young people in both AME Church activities and interdenominational fellowship. In 1900, the AME bishops recommended that the Reverend Benjamin W. Arnett Jr. be appointed as the league's general secretary (R. R. Wright, *Encyclopaedia of the African Methodist Episcopal Church*, 328). In the wake of the death of Arnett's father, the Reverend Benjamin W. Arnett Sr., on October 7, 1906, Carter referred to him as her "benefactor in the lecture field" (April 1907, 382), and she may well have assisted the younger Arnett in organizing leagues around the country. The *Encyclopaedia of the African Methodist Episcopal Church* makes no mention of Carter's work on behalf of the Allen Christian Endeavor League, instead lauding the Reverend E. J. Greg and the Reverend Julian C. Caldwell for their efforts, which resulted the creation of 4,125 leagues with 150,000 members by 1915.

17. Anna Julia Cooper, *The Voice of Anna Julia Cooper, Including A Voice from the South and Other Important Essays, Papers, and Letters*, ed. Charles Lemert and Esme Bhan (Rowman & Littlefield, 1998), 92–94. In "Woman Versus the Indian," published in *A Voice from the South* (1892), Cooper notes especially conductors who assist white women travelers while turning their backs on Black women. She also wonders whether she belongs in the waiting room marked "For Ladies" or the one "For Colored People." (94). That said, she notes that conductors do not make the laws but merely enforce them (94). Writing in 1891 and 1892, Ida B. Wells complains that separate-car laws mean that Black travelers, "regardless of advancement," must ride in "filthy, stifling partitions cut off from smoking cars" (*The Light of Truth: Writings of an Anti-Lynching Crusader*, ed. Mia Bay [Penguin, 2014], 31–32, 69).

18. See Bay, *To Tell the Truth Freely*, 46. See also Mia Bay, *Traveling Black: A Story of Race and Resistance* (Belknap Press of Harvard University Press, 2021), esp. chap. 2, "Traveling by Train: The Jim Crow Car"; Amy G. Richter, *Home on the Rails: Women, the Railroad, and the Rise of Public Domesticity* (University of North Carolina Press, 2005), esp. chap. 3, "At Home Aboard: Railway Travel and the Rise of Public Domesticity."

19. For more on Carter's travels through Florida, see Cynthia Patterson, "The Florida Trail in Black (Not White), 1903–1912," *Journal of Florida Studies* 1:9

(2021): https://www.journaloffloridastudies.org/files/vol0109/patterson-florida-trail-black.pdf.

20. See Larry Tye, *Rising from the Rails: Pullman Porters and the Making of the Black Middle Class* (Holt, 2004).

21. I am indebted to Dr. Alexandra Cornelius of Florida International University for suggesting an ironic reading of these passages. Dr. Cornelius served as commentator for the 2018 panel at the African American Intellectual History Society conference at which I initially presented this research.

22. In 1899, Florida had a scant seventeen hundred miles of rail line, most of it short routes connecting smaller towns and cities (Charlton W. Tebeau and William Marina, *A History of Florida* [University of Miami Press, 1999], 266).

23. Du Bois contributed two articles to the *Review* during this period: "The Present Outlook for the Darker Races of Mankind" (October 1900), and "The Problem of Work" (October 1903).

24. Du Bois, "Of the Black Belt," 439. For Du Bois's government and academic publications, see W. E. B. Du Bois, *Contributions by W. E. B. Du Bois in Government Publications and Proceedings*, comp. Herbert Aptheker (Kraus-Thomson, 1980); and W. E. B. Du Bois, *Atlanta University Publications* (4 vols.; Octagon Books, 1968–69).

25. Du Bois, "Of the Black Belt," 439–55.

26. Du Bois, "Of the Black Belt, 439."

27. The *Review* published five essays contributed by Washington in this era: "Taking Advantage of Our Disadvantages" (April 1894); "The American Negro of To-Day" (April 1908); "The Basis of Ascendancy" (July 1910); "Industrial Education and Negro Progress" (January 1913"; and "The Mission Work of the Negro Church" (January 1916), which appeared after his December 14, 1915, death. See also Booker T. Washington, *Character Building: Being Addresses Delivered on Sunday Evenings to the Students of Tuskegee Institute* (Doubleday, Page, 1903). Washington's book reportedly had "immense sale in both this country and Europe" (La Salle A. Maynard, "Books and Authors," *Frank Leslie's Weekly*, March 26, 1903).

28. Washington, *Character Building*, 57–62; Wells, *Light of Truth*, 36.

29. "Allen, Mrs. Phoebe C.," in *Centennial Encyclopaedia*, 22.

30. W. E. B. Du Bois, *Writings* (Literary Classics of the United States, 1986), 834–39.

31. The practice of providing magazine artwork suitable for pulling out and framing was a well-established practice dating back at least to the mass circulation of American periodicals in the nineteenth-century. See Cynthia Lee Patterson, *Art for the Middle Classes: America's Illustrated Magazines of the 1840s* (University Press of Mississippi, 2010).

32. Larry Eugene Rivers and Canter Brown Jr.'s excellent history, *Laborers in the Vineyard of the Lord: The Beginnings of the AME Church in Florida, 1865–1895*

(University Press of Florida, 2001) does not mention Potter and these two churches, likely because they were built after 1895.

33. "St. John's African Methodist Episcopal (AME) Church," *Encyclopedia of Cleveland History*, accessed August 22, 2025, https://case.edu/ech/articles/s/st-johns-african-methodist-episcopal-ame-church; "St. John A.M.E. Church," Cleveland Boy Scouts—The Cleveland Central Rangers, accessed August 22, 2025, https://theuniqueclevelandcentralrangers.wordpress.com/about/st-john-a-m-e-church/.

34. "Bethel A.M.E. Church," *Baltimore Places*, accessed August 22, 2025, https://places.baltimoreheritage.org/bethel-ame-church/.

35. Lena Mason, 1900 US Census, Hannibal Ward 5, Marion, Missouri, roll 874, p. 1, ED 0104; *The Index* (Hermitage, Missouri), September 27, 1894; "Rev. Mrs. Lena Mason," *Fort Scott (Kansas) Daily Monitor*, March 21, 1899; "The Negro Chautauqua," *Owensboro (Kentucky) Messenger*, August 1, 1907; "Rev. Mrs. Lena Mason," *Kansas City (Missouri) Sun*, November 23, 1918. Jualynne E. Dodson mentions Mason but does not refer to her as "reverend" and notes that she "was so reluctant to believe that a woman could expound the gospel that she had to receive three calls to preach before responding positively" (Dodson, *Engendering Church*, 79). However, Dodson provides no sources for this information. Mason's entry in the African American Biographical Database (ProQuest Information and Learning, 2001–21) lists her as a member of the Colored Methodist Episcopal Church rather than the AME Church, but that assertion appears to be inaccurate. See D. W. Culp, ed., *Twentieth Century Negro Literature* (1902; Arno Press, 1969), 444–48. Although the AME denomination's centennial edition of the *Encyclopaedia* (1916) mentions "Mrs. Lena Mason," she is omitted from the 1948 version, which provides biographical sketches of many noted leaders, both men and women.

36. It is unclear whether Mason's case parallels the 1884 controversy over Turner's ordination of Sarah Ann Hughes or whether Carter simply misunderstood Mason's status: while women evangelists could be licensed to preach in the AME denomination, apparently only men could be ordained as ministers and employ the title *Reverend*. For the earlier controversy, see Angell and Pinn, *Social Protest Thought*, 268. Angell and Pinn claim that the AME Church did not ordain another woman until 1948, although several were licensed to preach (269). See also Stephen W. Angell, "The Controversy over Women's Ministry in the African Methodist Episcopal Church During the 1880s: The Case of Sarah Ann Hughes," in *This Far by Faith: Readings in African-American Women's Religious Biography*, ed. Judith Weisenfeld and Richard Newman (Routledge, 1996). Whatever the AME Church's official position, accounts of Mason's work in both the white and Black press consistently refer to her *Reverend*.

37. Though Carter *gives* the titles of some of her addresses, none of the texts are known to have been preserved.

38. Albert Blakeslee White, *Public Addresses of Albert Blakeslee White, A.M., Governor of West Virginia, During His Term of Office* (Tribune, 1905), 300.

Chapter 6: Matters Educational

1. Adam Fairclough, *A Class of Their Own: Black Teachers in the Segregated South* (Belknap Press of Harvard University Press, 2007), 189. See also James D. Anderson, *The Education of Blacks in the South, 1860–1935* (University of North Carolina Press, 1988); Sarah H. Case, *Leaders of Their Race: Educating Black and White Women in the New South* (University of Illinois Press, 2017).

2. Anderson, *Education of Blacks in the South*, 13. Little data is available about these local undertakings since they generally were not required to submit reports to local, state, or federal officials.

3. As Elizabeth Renker has demonstrated, as late as 1938, 60 percent of Black college graduates of both sexes entered teaching-related professions at the primary and secondary education level (*The Origins of American Literature Studies* [Cambridge University Press, 2007], 69).

4. McHenry, *Forgotten Readers*.

5. Heather Andrea Williams, *Self-Taught*, 5.

6. See, Muhammad, *Cultivating Genius*, esp. chap. 1, "How 19th-Century Black Literary Societies Can Elevate Today's Literacy Learning," and chap. 2, "What Is Historically Responsive Literacy?"

7. Johnson, Pitre, and Johnson, *African American Women Educators*; McCluskey, *Forgotten Sisterhood*.

8. Webster, *Beyond the Boundaries*, esp. chapter 4, "In School: The Journey to the Classroom and Equal Education," and chapter 5, "The World Their Parents Made: Activism and Discourse of Black Parents and Mothers."

9. Angell and Pinn, *Social Protest Thought*, 73.

10. J. H. Collett, *The Doctrines and Discipline of the African Methodist Episcopal Church*, comp. Benjamin F. Lee et al. (AME Book Concern, 1905).

11. Fairclough, *Class of Their Own*, 11. Based on the sixteenth-century French *école normale*, normal schools employed model classrooms and modeled teaching strategies. See Wendy A. Paterson, "From 1871 to 2021: A Short History of Education in the United States," Buffalo State University, December 8, 2021, https://suny.buffalostate.edu/news/1871-2021-short-history-education-united-states.

12. Carole Wylie Hancock, "Eminently Qualified," in *African American Women Educators*, ed. Johnson, Pitre, and Johnson, 1. Hancock provides a helpful overview of the previous scholarly literature on African American teachers. She notes that Darlene Clark Hine, ed., *Black Women in America* (2 vols.; Oxford University

Press, 2005), contains 113 biographical sketches of women educators, only one of whom, Frances Joseph, is discussed here.

13. "Mary Elizabeth Lembert" [sic], *Michigan, U.S., Death Records, 1867–1952* (database online), accessed November 18, 2019, Ancestry.com; Janet Gray, "Passing as Fact: Mollie E. Lambert and Mary Eliza Tucker Lambert Meet as Racial Modernity Dawns," *Representations* 64 (1998): 41–75; "Detroit Correspondence," *Christian Recorder*, January 30, 1869; "Word from Detroit," *Christian Recorder*, May 3, 1877; "The Ladies of the Queen of Shela [sic]," *Christian Recorder*, April 19, 1877. As Gray points out, several scholars of nineteenth-century American literature have conflated or confused Mollie Lambert with a white author, Mary Eliza Lambert. Mollie Lambert also edited a publication, *The Progressive Age*, sponsored by the AME Sunday school, and was a frequent contributor to *The Christian Recorder*; see, for example, "Bon Tons" (August 16, 1877), "Missions—Home and Foreign" (August 23, 1877), "Word from Detroit" (September 6, 1877), "A Dream of Heaven" (September 13, 1877), "A Trip to Toledo" (October 18, 1877), "An Evening with Bunyan" (November 29, 1877), "A Word for Our Boys" (October 5, 1882), "A Christmas Story" (December 1882), and "Twilight Musings" (October 2, 1884).

14. The earliest known issue of the *A.M.E. Church Review* is dated July 1884 and is labeled volume 1. However, the AME Church website reports that the *Review* was simply an extension and renaming of an earlier publication, *The AME Magazine*, edited by the Reverend George Hogarth See http://www.ame-historyinthemaking.com/the-a-m-e-review/, accessed November 25, 2019). Since *The Christian Recorder*, January 21, 1884, published the "Contents for the January Number" of the *Review*, the quarterly likely began publication earlier than July 1884. Earlier issues of the *Magazine* and the *Review* have not been located.

15. The article that prompted Lambert was likely D. Augustus Straker's "The Congo Valley: Its Redemption" (January 1884). Straker's article apparently argued that in spite of the horrors of slavery in the West Indies and America, African-descended people retained mental capacities associated with their ancestors in the Congo (*Christian Recorder*, January 21, 1884).

16. Women teachers spent an average of 2.5 years in the profession, and most ended their careers when they married (Hancock, "Eminently Qualified," 15).

17. *Christian Recorder*, June 6, 1878; Hannah Jones, *Philadelphia, Pennsylvania, Marriage Index, 1885–1951* (database online), accessed December 6, 2019, Ancestry.com; Hannah J. Brown, 1910 US Census, Philadelphia Ward 26, Philadelphia, Pennsylvania, roll T624_1401, p. 11b, ED 0586. According to Coppin, *Reminiscences*, 167, Jones remained principal for eighteen years and resigned when she married Brown. However, the marriage took place in 1908, and Jones is still listed as a teacher in the 1910 US Census, though it does not indicate where she was employed.

18. Samuel P. Orth, *A History of Cleveland, Ohio* (S. J. Clarke, 1910), 1:539. See also Jane H. Freeman, *U.S. City Directories, 1822–1995* (database online), accessed November 19, 2019, Ancestry.com. Andreá Williams has written about single Black women in "Searching for Singles: Archival Approaches for Singleness Studies and Black Women's Collections," in *Single Lives: Modern Women in Literature, Culture, and Film*, ed. Katherine Fama and Jorie Lagerway (Rutgers University Press, 2022).

19. "Obituary, Mrs. Belle B. Dorce," *Christian Recorder*, February 26, 1891.

20. "A Factor in Human Progress" is reprinted in Harper, *Brighter Coming Day*, 275–80.

21. "Teaching as a Profession" and "A Plea for the Moral Aim in Education" are reprinted in Angell and Pinn, *Social Protest Thought*.

22. Dandridge, introduction, xxix; Alice E. Dunnigan, "Early History of Negro Women in Journalism," *Negro History Bulletin* 28:8 (1965): 178–79, 193, 197; Gloria Wade-Gayles, "Black Women Journalists in the South, 1880–1905: An Approach to the Study of Black Women's History," *Callaloo* 11/13 (1981): 138–52.

23. Mattie Roberts, 1880 US Census, Adrian, Lenawee, Michigan, roll 590, p. 56c, ED 147; "Adrian College," *Chicago Tribune*, June 26, 1885; W. D. Johnson, "Wilberforce University—Her Greatest Commencement," *Christian Recorder*, July 10, 1890; W. H. S. Seals, "Wilberforce Quarto-Centennial," *Christian Recorder*, August 16, 1888; "Miss Mattie Roberts, Retired Teacher, Dead," *Indianapolis News*, February 1, 1936.

Chapter 7: Matters Scientific and Philosophical

1. Britt Rusert, *Fugitive Science: Empiricism and Freedom in Early African American Culture* (New York University Press, 2017), 5.

2. See, for example, "Nuts and Fruit for Brain Work" (April 1902); "Food Mixtures to Avoid" (July 1903); "Take Care of Your Health" and "The Best Physical Culture" (October 1902); "The Science of Diet" (April 1904); "A Question of Diet" (January 1901); "Cooking by the Clock" (October 1899); "Oysters and Disease" (April 1902); "Best Way to Treat a Sprain" (October 1899); "Radium as a Cancer Cure" (October 1903).

3. Darlene Clark Hine, "Co-Laborers in the Work of the Lord: Nineteenth-Century Black Women Physicians," in *"Send Us a Lady Physician,"* ed. Abram, 110.

4. Family tree, "Dr. Hallie E. Tanner Dillon Johnson," Ancestry.com, accessed November 28, 2019; "In this Issue Wilberforce and Bethel University Make Announcements," *Christian Recorder*, May 14, 1891; "Doctor Hallie T. Dillon," *Cawker City (Kansas) Public Record*, November 26, 1891; "Mrs. Hallie Q. Dillon," *Times-Picayune* (New Orleans), April 20, 1892.

5. Hine, "Co-Laborers in the Work of the Lord," 108; Jasmin K. Williams, "Dr. Susan Smith McKinney Steward," *New York Amsterdam News*, March 14–20, 2013;

"Obituary, McKinney, Rev. Wm. G.," *Christian Recorder*, December 20, 1894; Susan S. McKinney, *New York City, Compiled Marriage Index, 1600s–1800s* (database online), accessed November 29, 2019, Ancestry.com.; Hallie Q. Brown, "Dr. Susan S. (McKinney) Steward," in *Homespun Heroines*, 162–63; Susan McKinney Smith Steward, Find a Grave, accessed July 26, 2025, https://www.findagrave.com/memorial/3350/susan-mckinney-steward. The US Census records for 1860 correctly identify the other members of Steward's extended household and list her age as eighteen, which would indicate that she was born in 1842. However, the 1880 US Census records her age as thirty-three, which would indicate that she was born in 1847. Moreover, the *Directory of Deceased American Physicians, 1804–1929* ([database online], accessed July 27, 2025, Ancestry.com) lists her birthdate as January 22, 1845. The 1875 New York State Census gives her age as thirty-five, indicating that she was born in 1840 (Susan McKinney, *Census of the State of New York, 1875* [database online], accessed July 26, 2025, Ancestry.com). Brown, "Dr. Susan S. (McKinney) Steward," lists Steward's birth year as 1848, while Jasmin K. Williams, "Dr. Susan Smith McKinney Steward," reports that Steward was born in March 1847.

6. Mamie Jarvis may have been Mary E. Parker, the mother of Joseph Wentworth Jarvis, an AME minister who was born on July 11, 1872, in Antigua, and who was serving a congregation in Pittsburgh, Pennsylvania, in 1923 when he contributed to the July 1923 issue of the *Review*. See Joseph Wentworth Jarvis death certificate, December 29, 1944, *Pennsylvania, U.S., Death Certificates, 1906–1972* (database online), accessed 21 September 2024, Ancestry.com.

7. Ruth Brinson, 1880 US Census, Xenia, Greene, Ohio, roll 1019, p. 400c, ED 090; *Xenia (Ohio) Daily Gazette*, February 19, 1891, August 8, 1896, April 19, 1898, July 20, August 1, 1903; *Christian Recorder*, September 1, December 8, 22, 1898; *Dayton (Ohio) Herald*, April 21, 1899; "Tract 3," *Washington C.H. Record-Herald* (Ohio), March 20, 1939; *Dayton (Ohio) Daily News*, November 22, 1918; "Retired Teacher Dies at Xenia," *Journal Herald* (Dayton, Ohio), December 8, 1960.

8. Johnson later served as editor of *The Christian Recorder*, 1893–1902 (*Encyclopedia.com*, "Christian Recorder," accessed December 6, 2019, https://www.encyclopedia.com/history/encyclopedias-almanacs-transcripts-and-maps/christian-recorder). Lavatt was a member of the Ontario, Canada, AME Conference (James W. Lavatt, "A.M.E. Conference Canada," *Christian Recorder*, July 31, 1890). Jordan was a traveling agent for Atlanta's Morris Brown College (J. A. Lindsay, "Morris Brown College," *Christian Recorder*, June 7, 1894).

9. See *Stanford Encyclopedia of Philosophy*, "Natural Philosophy in the Renaissance," accessed December 6, 2019, https://plato.stanford.edu/entries/natphil-ren/.

10. G. Stanley Hall, "Philosophy in the United States," *Mind* 4:13 (1879): 89–105.

11. Sylvanie Williams in the 1870 US Census; Sylvia Williams in the 1880 US Census; Sylvinie Williams in the 1900 US Census; Sylvania Williams in the 1920

US Census; *Weekly Louisianian* (New Orleans), March 26, 1881; "Announcement," *Town Talk* (Alexandria, Louisiana), June 7, 1897; *Times-Picayune* (New Orleans), September 29, 1892, March 18, 1894; "Several Speakers Tell What Afro-American May Accomplish in Marts of Trade," *Times-Democrat* (New Orleans), July 7, 1910; "Delegates Are Named by Hall," *Daily Signal* (Crowley, Louisiana), March 29, 1916; Sylvanie Francoz Williams, *New Orleans, Louisiana, Death Records Index, 1804–1949* (database online), accessed December 1, 2019, Ancestry.com.

12. See William Ladd, *An Essay on a Congress of Nations for the Adjustment of International Disputes Without Resort to Arms* (1840; Oxford University Press, 1916).

13. Bailey Haeussler, "Julia Caldwell Frazier: Pioneering African-American Educator," *Handbook of Texas*, August 30, 2022, https://www.tshaonline.org/handbook/entries/frazier-julia-caldwell; Hollis Robbins and Henry Louis Gates Jr., eds., *The Portable Nineteenth-Century African American Women Writers* (Penguin Books, 2017), 483; Julia L. Caldwell, *U.S. City Directories, 1822–1995* (database online), accessed December 1, 2019, Ancestry.com; "Noted Educator Addresses 1,000 Negro Teachers in Session Here," *Marshall (Texas) News Messenger*, December 1, 1928.

14. Linda M. Perkins, "Heed Life's Demands: The Educational Philosophy of Fanny Jackson Coppin," *Journal of Negro Education* 51:3 (1982): 181–90. For more on Coppin, see Linda M. Perkins, *Fanny Jackson Coppin and the Institute for Colored Youth* (Garland, 1987). Catherine Casey contributed sixteen "Woman's Department" or "Women's Department" columns to *The Christian Recorder*, including one that identifies Casey as Coppin. All but one were published in 1878; the one dated February 16, 1888, may be a typographical error, since it seems unlikely that Coppin continued to rely on the pseudonym ten years later, especially since material appeared under her real name during that time. Catherine Casey also contributed two fictional works to the *Recorder*: "A New Year's Story" (January 3, 10, 1878), and "Uncle Davy's Christmas Story" (December 26, 1878).

15. Edna D. Gullins, 1930 US Census, Philadelphia, Pennsylvania, p. 27a, ED 0734; Helen M. Hunt, "Among Our Colored Citizens," *Delaware County Daily Times* (Chester, Pennsylvania), June 11, 1946; R. R. Wright, *Encyclopaedia* of the African Methodist Episcopal *Church*, 124; "WIL to Hear Noted Women at Luncheon," *Altoona Tribune* (Pennsylvania), November 12, 1946.

16. "WILPF History," WILPF: Women's International League for Peace & Freedom, accessed July 27, 2025, https://www.wilpf.org/history/. The first mention of Gullins's affiliation with the organization appeared in "WIL to Hear Noted Women at Luncheon."

Conclusion: Writing Race Literature in Extraordinary Times

1. Henderson, *Doctrine and Discipline*, 110, stipulated that preachers should not be permitted to remain at one location for longer than five years except in "extreme cases of necessity."

Index

Page numbers in **bold** indicate illustrations.

abolitionism: *The Colored American*, 26; Dickens's views, 26
"Action for the Hour" (Williams), 136–38
Addams, Jane, 65
"Advantages of Beginning Trades in Our Schools and Colleges, The" (Straker), 116
"Afmerica" (Lee), 47
African Methodist Episcopal (AME) Church: AME Book Concern, 9; *Doctrine and Discipline*, 23, 35, 117; ministry, calling to, 60; ministry, itinerant model, 143, 175n1; mission work, 40; patriarchal leadership structure, 143; print media established by, 9–10; *Voice of Missions*, 53; women's evangelism, 62; *Women's Missionary Recorder*, 46; Women's Mite Missionary Society, 49, 60, 68, 81; women's roles, 51, 108, 143
African Methodist Episcopal Church Magazine, 90
Afro-American Council, 5
"Afro American Poets and Their Verse" (Tillman), 22–23, 46
"Afro-American Woman in Verse, The" (Mossell), 45
"Afro-American Women and Their Work" (Tillman), 46, 50–52
Alabama State Normal School for Negroes, 102
alcohol consumption, 75–80
Aldridge, Delores P., 14, 55
"Alexandre Dumas, Pére" (Tillman), 29–30
"Alexander Pope" (Lake), 29
"Alexander Sergeivich Pushkin" (Tillman), 29, 30–31
Allen, G. W., 101
Allen, Phoebe Harvey, 101
Allen, Richard, 9, 49
Allen, Sarah, 49
Allen Christian Endeavor League, 93, 105, 110, 167n16
AME Church Magazine, The, 9
A.M.E. Church Review, The, **54**; artistic culture, 37–39; as cultural space for criticism and analysis,

17–18; educational functions, 114–24; evangelism, 155n5; foundation and goals, 4, 6, 10–11; gender issues addressed in content, 8–9; historical essays, 40–52; literary biography, 25–31; literary criticism and book reviews, 31–35; literary histories, 20–25; male editors' views on women's roles, 56–58; poetry, 20–23; racial uplift as theme, 116; subscription agents, 87–88, 93–94; translations, 36–37; wider audience of, 109–10; women's contributions, exclusive issue (1901), 3–5; women's contributions, expanding, 8–9, 11–12; women's roles in home and church, 58–63. *See also* Coppin, Levi J.; Kealing, Hightower T.; "Notes of Travel" (Carter); Ransom, Reverdy C.; Tanner, Benjamin T.
American Journal of Sociology, 72
American Missionary Association, 103, 115
American Missionary Society, 19
"American Notes for General Circulation" (Dickens), 26
American Peace Society, 138
American Social Science Association, 78
American Sociological Society, 55
"Analysis of Science, Philosophy and Theology, An" (Jones), 134
Anderson, Mrs. W. T., 77, 78
Angell, Stephen W., 115
"Architecture in the A.M.E. Church" (feature column), 104
archival material, availability of, 142, 144
Armstrong, Lulu, 49
Arnett, Benjamin Williams, 48, 112
Arnett, Mary Louise, 48, **48**
"At Gettysburg" (Gullins), 140–41

Atlanta Congress of Colored Women, 79–80
Attucks, Crispus, 41–42
author's methodology, 12–16; archival material, availability of, 142, 144
Autobiography of Amanda Berry Smith, 88
"Awakening of Women, The" (Williams), 65

Ballard Normal School, 102–3, **103**
Baltimore, Anna, 49
Baltimore, Maryland, Bethel Church, 105–6
Baptist periodicals, 6
Baptist Young People's Union, 110–11
Barnett, Steven R., 36
Bay, Mia, 8, 78, 90
"Beauties in Evangeline" (Thompson), 33–34
Bellamy, Edward, 133
Bentley, Fannie C., 45, 47–49
Bethel Church, Baltimore, 105–6
Bethune, Mary McLeod, 115
Beyond Respectability (Cooper), 45
Bierce, Sarah Cordelia, 18–19
Biglow Papers (Lowell), 135–36
biobibliography, 153n15
birth rates for Black women, 128–29
Black, Luke, 98
Black landowning, 72–73
Black literature, 25
Black Newspaper and the Chosen Nation, The (Fagan), 6–7
Black Print Unbound (Gardner), 6
Black-owned businesses, 98–99, 100–104
Blackshear, E. L., 116
Bookwalter, John, 133–34
Boston, Watch and Ward Society, 66
Boston Massacre, 42

boycotts to protest segregation, 89–90
Bragg, Lucinda B., 37
Bright, Lemuel W., 96
Brinson, James F., 130
Brinson, Louisa, 130
Brinson, Ruth (Gales), 130–31
Broad Ax, The (Black newspaper), 82
Brown, Charlotte Hawkins, 115
Brown, Hallie Q., 48
Brown, Howard D., 120
Brown, Sarah D., 76–77
Brown, W. L., 116
Browning, Elizabeth Barrett, 21, 22
Buckbee, Mrs. C. M., 107
"Bunch of Pansies, A" (Lambert), 118
Burns, Harry T., 69
Burroughs, Nannie Helen, 115
Bustill, Gertrude E. H. *See* Mossell, Gertrude E. H. Bustill

Cable, George Washington, 34–35
Caldwell, Julia L., 138–39
Campbell, Frazelia, 32, 135–36
Campbell, Jabez Pitt, 139
Campbell, Julia, 32
Campbell, Mary A., 49, **49**
Carnegie, Andrew, 134
Carter, Dark, 98
Carter, Effie B., 67–68
Carter, E. Marie, 13, 14–15; background and education, 92; *Missionary Searchlight*, **93**; as subscription agent, 87–88, 93–94, 111–12. *See also* "Notes of Travel" (Carter)
Carter, J. E., 116
Casey, Catherine (pseudonym), 139. *See also* Coppin, Fanny Jackson
Chapman, Katherine Davis. *See* Tillman, Katherine Davis Chapman
Chappelle, Rosina Palmer, 60–61
Chappelle, William D., 60

Character Building (Washington), 100
"Charles Dickens" (Turpin), 25–26
"Charles Lamb" (Ray), 26–27
Cheeks, Mattie, 49
Chicago, Illinois: Louise Juvenile Home for Dependent Boys, 82; West Side Woman's Club, 82
Chicago World's Fair (1893), 64
child labor, 72
childless marriages, 62–63
Christian Culture Congress, 107
Christian Endeavor movement, 130
Christian Herald, The (newspaper), 9
Christian Index, The (periodical), 142
Christian Recorder, The (AME newspaper), 9, 46, 90, 118, 121; "The New Race Name, Afro-American," 47; "Woman's Department," 57, 139
"Christmas Eve" (Tieck), 36–37
Church, Lucy W., 49
Church of England Temperance Society, 80
citizenship, practice of, 13
Clark, Molliston M., 90
classical education, 116, 123, 135, 136
Class of Their Own, A (Fairclough), 114
class stratification, 8, 50, 65, 89, 130
Clayton, Robert, 23
Coakley, Rosetta Evelyn (Lawson), 75, **79**, 79–80
co-education, 123
"Co-Laborers in the Work of the Lord" (Hine), 128
Coleman, Lucretia H., 48
"College-Bred Negro, The" (Scarborough), 117
Collins, Ira, 105
Collins, Patricia Hill, 14, 55
"color question," 70–75
Colored American, The (newspaper), 26, 46

Colored Conventions Project, 88
Colored Orphan Asylum, New York City, 66
"Colored Woman in Verse, The" (Mossell), 24, 45
"Colored Women and the Suffrage" (Forbes), 69
Cooper, Albert B., 125
Cooper, Anna Julia, 14, 55, 82, 89; and feminist thought, 58
Cooper, Brittney C., 8, 12, 45, 64
Coppin, Fanny Jackson, 3, 42, 48, 57, 66, 112, 139–40
Coppin, Levi J., 4, 10–11, **11**, 112; book review columns, 31; education-related articles, 115–16; philosophical essays published, 134; travel, accounts of, 90–91; on women's roles, 57
Cottrell, Catherine, 101
Cottrell, Elias, 101
Council, William Hooper, 102
"Creation of the World Opposed to the Theory of Natural Philosophy" (Lavatt), 134
crime: and prison reform, 81–86; temperance and criminality, 75–80
"Crispus Attucks Monument, The" (Earle), 41–42

Dammond, William H., 117
Dandridge, Rita B., 20
Darwin, Charles, 139
de Lamartine, Alphonse, 36
"Decisions of Time, The" (Caldwell), 138–39
Deegan, Mary Jo, 55–56, 65
Delaney, A. D., 116
Denver Daily News, The (newspaper), 85
dialect verse, 22, 135
Dickerson, C. Hatfield, 57

Dickerson, Selena C. Gaines, 67
"Die Beiden Piccolomini" (Campbell), 32
Dillon, Charles E., 128
Dillon, Halle Tanner, 125, 128
Dillon, Sadie, 128
"Disciplinary Course of Study, The" (feature column), 117
divorce, 60
Dixon, Thomas, Jr., 86
Doctrine and Discipline of the AME Church, The, 23, 35, 117
"Do Negroes Constitute a Race of Criminals?" (Jackson), 84–85
Doolin, Lena (Mason), 108, **109**
Dorce, Belle, 114, 121
Dorce, Solomon George, 121
Dougan, Madam, 49
Douglass, Frederick, 4, 5
Dr. Sevier (Cable), 34–35
Drummond, Henry, 34
Du Bois, W. E. B., 4, 12, 52; at Atlanta University, 116; on purpose of higher education, 102; *The Souls of Black Folk*, 90, 98; Talented Tenth, 143; travel in Georgia, 98
Dumas, Alexandre, 29–30, 72
Dunbar, Paul Lawrence, 22
"Duties of a Primary Teacher, The" (Freeman), 120–21
"Dying Christian to His Soul, The" (Pope), 29

Earle, Victoria, 41–42
"Eastern Song, An" (Pushkin), 30–31
"Echoes from the 12th Episcopal District" (Taylor), 112
education: art and music, 123–24; classical education, 116, 123, 135, 136; co-education, 123; higher education, 101–3, 116; kindergartens,

121; progressive methods, 121–22; schools in Black communities, 114
"Educators of Literary Taste, The" (Potter/Yates), 126
Eighteenth Amendment, 75
Elliott, G. M., 116, 122
Ellis, Leonora Beck, 72–73, **73**
Emerson Industrial Home, 107
Encyclopaedia of the African Methodist Episcopal Church (Wright), 112
"engaged-sociology," 55
"Engineering Courses for our Colleges and Universities" (Dammond), 117
English language, history of, 18
engraving, mezzotint, 9–10
Evans, Mary, 108
"Experiences and Observations in the Black Belt" (Pemberton), 70

"Factor in Human Progress, A" (Harper), 116, 122
Fagan, Benjamin, 6–7
Fairclough, Adam, 114, 117
feminism, 57–58; pious feminism, 57–59, 64, 67, 77. *See also* women's roles
"Fetes for the Czar in Paris" (Noble), 41
"Field of Golden Grain or a Harvest of Rank Weeds, A" (Coppin), 139–40
Fielder, Brigitte, 64
Fields, Joe, 98
First Congress of Colored Women, 4
Fish, Cheryl J., 88
Fisher, Dorothy Canfield, 63
Fisk School for Girls, 136
Florida: AME district conferences, 93; church architecture, 104; in "Notes of Travel" (Carter), 94–95, 96–97
Forbes, George W., 31, 69, 126
Ford, Robert E., 110
Foreman, P. Gabrielle, 20
Fortune, T. Thomas, 4

Foster, Frances Smith, 4
France: African American residents, 71–72; French language, history of, 19; French literature, 24–25
Frazier, Charles Wales Wellington, 138
Frazier, Susan Elizabeth, 45–46
Frederick Douglass' Paper (periodical), 75–76
"Freedman's Triumphant Song, The" (Whitman), 23
Freedmen's Bureau, 103
Freeman, Jane H., 120
Freeman, Nellie, 114, 119, 120–21
"From the Field" (Coppin), 90–91
Fugitive Science (Rusert), 125
"Function of Language in the Secondary and the Higher Education, The" (Lightfoot), 117

Gaines, Julia A., 48, **48**
Gaines, Mary L., 49
Gaines, Wesley John, 48
Gaines, Willie Turner Gussie, 49
Gales, Ruth Brinson, 130–31
Gales, Winston A., 131
Gardner, Eric, 6, 90, 153n14
Garnet, Esta, 47
Gaudet, Adolph P., 81
Gaudet, Frances Joseph, 80, **80**, 81–82
gender roles. *See* women's roles
Georgia, African American land ownership, 72–73
Gettysburg battlefield, 140–41
Goddard, J. N., 125
Gohagen, Harrison, 98
Great Migration, 73–75, 134, 143
"Greatest Pictures of the World, The" (Johnson), 38
Greatest Thing in the World, The (Drummond), 34, 35
Green, Victor H., 14, 88

Green Book (film), 88
Green-Book, 14–15, 88–89, 113
Greene, Laura B., 48
Greene, Sherman Lawrence, 48
Greener, R. T., 5
Grimké, Charlotte, 22
Grube Method, 121
Gullins, Edna Dredden, 140–41
Gullins, William R., 140

Hack, Daniel, 25
Hackley, Emma Azalia, 71–72
Hall, G. Stanley, 62–63, 120–21
Hamilton, Mrs., 49
Hancock, Carole Wylie, 118
Handy, James A., 60
Handy, Mary A., 60, **61**
"Harmony Between the Bible and Science Concerning Primitive Man, The" (Williams), 125
Harper, Frances Ellen Watkins, 7, 14, 15, 22, 75–77, 116; "A Factor in Human Progress," 122; and feminist thought, 58; social reform, 66; on train and streetcar travel, 89; on Woman's Christian Temperance Union, 45
Hart, Lizzie, 90
"Has Christianity Benefitted Women?" (Stanton), 32–33
Haywood, Chanta M., 81
health, physical, 130; hygiene and sanitary science, 127
Heard, Josephine, 22, 47
Hemans, Felicia, 21
Hendricks, Wanda A., 64
"Henry Wadsworth Longfellow" (Tanner), 27–28
higher education, 101–3, 116
"Higher or Industrial Education" (Delaney), 116

Hine, Darlene Clark, 128
Hints on the Care of Children (Hubert), 65
"Home-Maker, The" (Lee), 58–59
homeopathic medicine, 129
homeownership, 100–101
"How the Color Question Looks to an American in France" (Hackley), 71–72
Howard University, 139
Howe, Mary W., 77–78
Howells, William Dean, 22
Hubert, Ellwood G., 65
Hubert, Lucy Williams, 65, **66**
Hugo, Victor, 76
Hull House, Chicago, 65
Hunter Institute, Louisiana, 101
hygiene and sanitary science, 127

"Indian Question," 77
Indian Territory, 97, 111
Indianapolis Freeman, The (Black periodical), 42
"Industrial Education the Need of Our Youth" (Jackson), 116
Industrial Home Association, 81
Institute for Colored Youth, Philadelphia, 32, 42, 46, 48, 57, 119
intemperance, 77–78. *See also* temperance movement
Inter Ocean, The (newspaper), 82
International Women's Congress, 140
"Is Education Generic?" (Mitchell), 116
"Is Higher Education Advantageous to the Negro?" (Carter), 116
"Is There a Conflict Between Religion and Science?" (Goddard), 125
Iverson, J. Oscar, 105

Jacks, John, 4
Jackson, Andrew, 102

Jackson, E. Belle, 107
Jackson, Ida Joyce, 84–86, **85**
Jackson, John Henry, 84
Jackson, Will M., 116
Jarvis, Mamie, 130, 173n6
Jewish travel guides, 88
Johnson, Andrew N., 38
Johnson, Benjamin Tanner, 128
Johnson, Dr. H. T. (*Christian Recorder* editor), 23
Johnson, Hallie Tanner, 28
Johnson, Henry T., 128, 134
Johnson, James H. A., 57
Johnson, John Quincy, 128
Johnson, John Quincy, Jr., 128
Johnson, Karen A., 115
Johnson, Kenneth L., 115
Johnson, Lillian J., 38
Johnson, Mr. and Mrs. James W., 97
Johnston, Mrs. Andrew N., 37, 38
Jones, Fredericka, 48
Jones, Hannah, 114, 119–20
Jones, J. A. M., 134
Jordan, D. J., 134
Joseph, Frances (Gaudet), 66, 80, **80**, 81–82

Kansas City Rising Sun, The (Black periodical), 42
Kasler, Dirk, 55
Kealing, Hightower T., 3–4; on A.M.E. Church architecture, 104; appeal for subscriptions (1909), 91, **91**; background, 6; book review columns, 31; commitment to women's contributions, 5; "The Disciplinary Course of Study," 117; on Dunbar's poetry, 22; on E. Marie Carter as subscription agent, 87; editing notes, 82, 84; editorship, 10–11, **11**, 25; educational background, 116–17; education-related articles, 116; first *A.M.E. Church Review* issue edited (1896), 53; format revisions of the *A.M.E. Church Review*, 53–54; philosophical essays published, 134; reprinted articles, 72; science department, 126; on women's contributions, 12
Kellor, Frances, 74
kindergartens, 121

Ladd, William, 138
Ladies' Home Journal (periodical), 46
Ladner, A. E., 95
Lake, Selena C., 29
Lamb, Charles, 26–27
Lamb, Mary, 26–27
Lambert, Mary Elizabeth Lewis, 47, 118–19
Lambert, Toussaint L'Ouverture, 118
"Land of the Czar" (Potter/Yates), 126
Laney, Lucy Craft, 48, 115
Langston, John Mercer, 37
Lavatt, James W., 134
Lawson, Jesse, 79
Lawson, Rosetta Evelyn Coakley, 75, **79**, 79–80
Layten, Sarah Willie, 73–74
Lee, Benjamin F., 47, 58
Lee, Mary Elizabeth Ashe, 47, **49**, 58–59
Lee, Mattie, 107
"Lessons from the Life of McKinley" (Washington), 26, 43–44
"Life and Literature" (Mossell), 23–24
Lightfoot, George M., 117
Lincoln, Abraham, 44–45
"Lincoln, the Emancipator" (Washington), 44–45
Lincoln Institute, Missouri, 126
"Lines of Negro Education" (Blackshear), 116

linguistics, 18
literacy, 114–15
literary criticism, 25–26
Lively Eight young people's club, 107
Living Way, The (Baptist periodical), 90
Lofton, Kathryn, 14, 40, 45
Longfellow, Henry Wadsworth, 22
Looking Backward (Bellamy), 133
Louise Juvenile Home for Dependent Boys, Chicago, 82
Louise Training School for Colored Boys, Chicago, 82
Louisiana Negro Business League, 137
Lowell, James Russell, 135–36
Luther, Martin, 42–43
lynch mobs, 86

Maffly-Kipp, Laurie F., 13–14, 40, 45
Mahorney, Gertrude Amelia, 36
Mann, Horace, 120
Mann, Mary Peabody, 120
"Marasmus Infantum" (McKinney), 129
"Marked Characteristics of the Negro Race, The" (White), 111
Martin Chuzzlewit (Dickens), 26
Martineau, Harriet, 55
Mason, George, 108
Mason, Lena Doolin, 108, **109**
Matthews, Victoria Earle, 4, 142
McCluskey, Audrey Thomas, 15, 115
McDonald, Elizabeth, 81, 82–84, **83**
McDonald, James, 82, 83
McDonald, Lynn, 55
McHenry, Elizabeth, 15, 114–15
McKinley, Ida, 80
McKinley, William, 43–44, 80
McKinney, Susan Smith, 128, 129, 172–73n5
McKinney, William G., 129
medical training, 128–29
Meyers, W. P., 109

mezzotint engravings, 9–10
Mill, Harriet Taylor, 55
Mill, John Stuart, 55
Miller, Mr. and Mrs. Percy, 101
"Milton's Satan" (Campbell), 33
"Minister's Wife, The" (Handy), 60
Missionary Chronicle, The (missionary society periodical), 118
Mississippi Industrial College, 101–2, **102**
Mitchell, S. T., 116
Monzon, P. M., 106
Moody, Joycelyn, 7, 17
Morris, Aldon D., 70–71
Mossell, Aaron Albert, 35
Mossell, Gertrude E. H. Bustill, 3, 35; "The Afro-American Council . . . ," 5; background, 46; "The Colored Woman in Verse," 24; historical writings, 47; "Life and Literature," 23–24; race histories, 45; "scrap-booking" style, 47
Mossell, Mary Louisa Tanner, review of *The Greatest Thing in the World*, 34, 35
Mossell, Nathan Francis, 35, 46
Mott, Frank Luther, 4
Muhammad, Gholdy, 15, 115
"Municipal Franchises" (Potter/Yates), 132–33
"Music, and Woman's Relation to It" (Bragg), 37–38
"Music in Education" (Scarborough), 124
Musical Messenger, The (music periodical), 37

Narrative of the Travels of Nancy Prince, 88
Nashville Globe, The (Black newspaper), 38
National Afro-American Council, 12

National Arbitration League, 138
National Association of Colored Women, 4, 12, 74, 84
National Baptist Magazine, The (periodical), 6
National Baptist Union-Review, The (periodical), 142
National League for the Protection of Colored Women, 74
National Negro Business League, 102
National Urban League, 74
National Woman Suffrage Association, 56
"National Woman's Christian Temperance Union" (Harper), 45, 76–77
"Natural Science in the Schools" (Potter/Yates), 125, 126–27
"Necessity of Higher Education, The" (Tunnell), 116
"Negro Among Anglo-Saxon Poets, The" (Tillman), 21–22, 46
Negro Motorist Green-Book, The (Green), 14–15, 88–89, 113
"Negro Problem," 77
Nell, William C., 5
Nelson, Alice Dunbar, 7
"New Education, The" (Dorce), 121
New Orleans Colored Teachers' League, 136
New York City, Colored Orphan Asylum, 66
New York Evening Post (newspaper), 53
New York Independent, The (magazine), 76
Newton, Charles Wesley, 92
Nightingale, Florence, 55
Nineteenth Amendment, 69
Noble, Mrs. H. R., 41
Northern Baptist Convention, 74
"Northern Phase of a Southern Problem, A" (Layten), 73–74

Norton, Charles Elliott, 28
"Notes of Travel" (Carter), 88–96; on Black-owned businesses, 98–99, 100–104; churches and parsonages, 104–6; demographic data, 99; feminized sociology in, 98–99; historical and geographical aspects, 96–99; humor, 98; racial harmony, promotion of, 109–13; as social column, 112; women, advocacy for, 106–8

"Official Service as a Probation Officer in the Cook County Juvenile Court" (McDonald), 83–84
Oklahoma Territory, 97
Old Creole Days (Cable), 34
"On Getting a Home" (Washington), 100
Othello (Shakespeare), 22
"Our Civil Rights" (Frazier), 46
Our Women and Children (magazine), 46
Overground Railroad, The (Taylor), 88

Packard, George Y., 28
Parker, Francis Wayland, 121–22
Parker, Mary E. (Mamie Jarvis), 130, 173n6
Path of Evolution Through Ancient Thought and Modern Science, The (Pemberton), 70
Payne, Daniel A., 9, 48, 139
Payne, Eliza J., 48
Peabody Normal School, 136
Pemberton, Caroline Hollingsworth, 70, **71**
Pemberton, Caroline Towne Hollingsworth, 70
Pemberton, Henry, 70
Pemberton, John C., 70
peonage system, 70

"Personal Work, the Demand of the Hour" (Carter), 111
Peterson, Carla L., 88
Philadelphia Council of Churches: Interracial Department, 140
Philadelphia Inquirer (newspaper), 46
Philadelphia Press (newspaper), 46
Philadelphia Times (newspaper), 46
Phillis Wheatley Club, 107
philosophy: philosophical essays, 125, 134–41; study of, 135
"Philosophy of Progress, The" (Jordan), 134
"Philosophy Religiously Valued" (Johnson), 134
"Physiology and Hygiene" (Potter/Yates), 125, 126, 127
Pinn, Anthony B., 115
pious feminism, 57–59, 64, 67, 77
Pitre, Abul, 115
"Plea for the Co-Education of the Sexes, A" (Washington), 122, 123
"Plea for the Moral Aim in Education, A" (Washington), 122
poetry: in the *A.M.E. Church Review*, 20–23; "The Afro-American Poets and Their Verse" (Tillman), 22–23, 66; "The Afro-American Woman in Verse" (Mossell), 45; "The Negro Among Anglo-Saxon Poets" (Tillman), 21–22, 46; "The Province of Poetry" (Turpin Washington), 20–21
"Political Results of the Reformation" (Yates), 42–43
Populist Party, 72
Potter, M. D., 104
Potter, R. K. (pseudonym), 42, 126. *See also* Yates, Josephine Silone
"Powerful Influence of Heredity, The" (Brinson), 130–31

"Practical Physiology" (Dillon), 125, 128–29
Price, Green, 110
prison reform, 81–86
"Prison Reform Work in New Orleans" (Joseph), 81–82
Progressive Era, 114, 152n7
Prohibition Party, 77
Protestant Reformation, 42–43
"Proverbial Philosophy of the Colored Race, The" (Jones), 134
"Province of Poetry, The" (Turpin Washington), 20–21
Provincial Freeman, The (newspaper), 75
pseudonyms, use of, 11–12, 126
"Purity of the Home" (Jackson), 84
Pushkin, Alexander, 29, 30–31

Quincy Method, 121

"race biographies," 43–45
"race histories," 45–52
race literature: calls for development of, 142; expanding range of, 6; Mossell on, 23–24; "The Value of Race Literature" (Matthews), 4–5; women's contributions, 8, 15
racial harmony, promotion of, 109–13
racial uplift, 88, 90, 116; and Black-owned businesses, 98–99, 100–104; and education, 114–15; and home-ownership, 100–101
racism, scientific, 70–71
Ransom, Reverdy C., 10, 67, 112; education-related articles, 116; literary criticism, 31; science department, 126; on social justice, 117
"Rape of the Lock" (Pope), 29
Ray, Charles Bennett, 26
Ray, H. Cordelia, 22, 47; "Charles Lamb," 26–27

Reformation, Protestant, 42–43
"Remedy for War, A" (Turpin Washington), 138
Repository of Religion and Literature and of Science and Art, The, 9–10, 90
"Requisites of True Leadership, The" (Wells), 100
"Responsibilities and Duties of the Women of the Twentieth Century, The" (Dickerson), 67
"Rice, Miss H. A." (pseudonym), 34–35
Rickett, Sallie, 107
rights, doctrine of, 68
Ringwood's Afro-American Journal of Fashion, 46
"River Systems of the United States" (Yates), 131–32
Roberts, Dr. and Mrs. D. P., 95–96
Roberts, Mattie F., 114, 123–24
Ronnick, Michele Valerie, 19
Roosevelt, Theodore, 68, 86
Ruffin, Josephine St. Pierre, 5
"Runaway Slave at Pilgrim's Point, The" (Browning), 22
Rural Versus Urban (Bookwalter), 133–34
"Rural Versus Urban" (Potter/Yates), 133–34
Rusert, Britt, 125
"Russia's New Literature" (Potter/Yates), 126

Samuel, Shirley, 20
Sanders, W. J., 96
"sanitary science," 127
Sartain, John, 9–10
Saturday Evening Post (periodical), 53
Scarborough, Sarah C. Bierce, 18–19, 124; translation work, 36
Scarborough, William Sanders, 19, 117
Schiller, Freidrich, 32

"Science Confirming the Scriptures" (Cooper), 125
science writing, 125–34
segregation, 70–71; boycotts in protest of, 89–90; on trains and streetcars, 89–90
Selika, Madame (Marie Selika Williams), 48
Senchyne, Jonathan, 64
"separate spheres," 57, 68
Shaffer, Cornelius T., 108
Shakespeare, William, 22
Sheridan, Moses, 92, 94
Sheridan, Philip, 92
Shorter, E. Marie, 48
Shorter, James A., 48
"Sixteenth Century in the Education of Modern Thought, The" (Campbell), 135–36
slavery, 76
Smith, Susan Maria, 129
social Darwinism, 70–71
Social Gospel movement, 67, 117
Social Protest Thought in the AME Church, 1862–1939 (Angell and Pinn), 115
social reform, 55, 142–43
sociology: "color question," 70–75; crime and prison reform, 81–86; "engaged-sociology," 55; expansions of research, turn of twentieth century, 55–56; "Notes of Travel" (Carter), 97–98; pre-sociology era, 54–55; social reform movements, 14, 64–67; sociological writing on home and family, 53–63; suffrage movement, 67–69; temperance and criminality, 75–80; University of Chicago graduate department, 56, 71; women's contributions to, 55–56, 159–60n3

"Some Afro-American Women of Mark" (Frazier), 45–46
Souls of Black Folk, The (Du Bois), 90, 98
Southern Christian Recorder, The (AME newspaper), 59, 101
"Southern Negro as a Property-Owner, The" (Ellis), 72–73
Southern Workman, The (Black periodical), 42
Spires, Derrick, 11–12, 13
spiritual autobiographies, 7
Staël, Madame Germaine de, 21
Stanton, Elizabeth Cady, 32–33
Star of Zion, The (AME periodical), 142
Stephen the Black (Pemberton), 70
stereotypes of Black people: Black church women, 7; in Black literature, 18
Steward, Susan Smith McKinney, 128, 129, 172–73n5
Steward, Theophilus Gould, 129
Straker, D. Augustus, 116
"Study of Thoreau, A" (Tanner), 27–28
"Suffrage in Illinois" (Williams), 68–69
suffrage movement, 67–69
Sunday schools, 120–21
syphilis, 129

"Tacitus' German Women" (Campbell), 32–33
Taggert, Miriam, 89
"Talented Tenth" (Du Bois), 52, 143
Tanner, Benjamin T., 10, 27, 59, 112, 128; book review columns, establishment of, 31; editorship, 10–11; education-related articles, 115; philosophical essays published, 134; on women's roles, 56–57
Tanner, Carl, 28
Tanner, Halle, 57, 125, 128
Tanner, Henry, 28
Tanner, Mary Louisa, 34, 35
Tanner, Sarah Elizabeth Miller, 27–28, 28, 35, 59, 128; "Henry Wadsworth Longfellow," 27–28; "A Study of Thoreau," 27–28
Tate, Claudia, 46, 50
Taylor, Candacy, 88
Taylor, G. E., 59
Taylor, Mrs. G. E., 59–60
Taylor, Nora F., 112
"Teaching as a Profession" (Washington), 122
temperance movement, 75–80; Prohibition, 75. *See also* Woman's Christian Temperance Union (WCTU)
"Temperance Reform a World-Wide Movement, The" (Lawson), 79–80
Terrell, Mary Church, 3, 89; "A Reply to a Statement Recently Made," 5
"Theosophy and the Theosophical School" (Potter/Yates), 126
Thomas, Edna C., 12
Thomas, J. Carrie, 49
Thompson, Lillian Viola, 32, 33–34
"Those Other People" (Gullins), 140
Tieck, Johann Ludwig, 36
Tillman, Ben, 86
Tillman, George M., 46
Tillman, Katherine Davis Chapman, 3, 18, 21–22, 45; "Afro-American Poets and Their Verse," 22–23; "Afro-American Women and Their Work," 50–52; background, 46; "Heirs of Slavery," 5; literary biographies, 29–30; race histories, 46; on women's roles in church, 61–62
Tom Watson's Magazine (Populist Party periodical), 72
Topeka Plaindealer, The (Kansas newspaper), 85

Toussaint-Louverture, 22, 36
"Toussaint L'Ouverture" (Whitter), 22
"true womanhood," 57
Tubman, Harriet, 112
Tunnell, W. V., 116
Turner, Eliza Ann, 48
Turner, Henry McNeal, 46, 48, 107, 112
Turner, Stephen, 54–55
Turpin, Josephine J. *See* Washington, Josephine J. Turpin
Tuskegee Institute, 102

Union Seminary, Wilberforce, 75
Unitarian Church, 76
University of Chicago: *American Journal of Sociology*, 72; sociology department, 56
Upshaw, Ida, 45, 49–50

"Value of a Classical Education, The" (Brown), 116
"Value of Race Literature, The" (Matthews), 4–5
vernacular speech patterns, 18
Voice of Missions (AME periodical), 53
Voice of the Negro, The (Black periodical), 42

Wade-Gayles, Gloria, 122
Wallenstein (Schiller), 32
Warner, Charles Dudley, 5
"Warning, The" (Longfellow), 22
Washington, Booker T., 4, 70, 100, 112, 117; controversy surrounding, 116; on purpose of higher education, 102; travels of, 90
Washington, Josephine J. Turpin, 18, 20, **21**, 138; "Charles Dickens," 25–26; on education, 122; "Lessons from the Life of McKinley," 26, 43–44; "Lincoln, the Emancipator," 44–45; "A Plea for the Moral Aim in Education," 117; "The Province of Poetry," 20–21; "What of the Children?," 62–63
Washington, Samuel Somerville Hawkins, 18, 43
Watch and Ward Society, Boston, 66
"We Must Educate" (Elliott), 116, 122
Webster, Crystal Lynn, 15, 115
Weekly Anglo African, The (newspaper), 76
Wells-Barnett, Ida B., 14, 55, 78–79, 89, 90; and feminist thought, 58; West Side Woman's Club, 82
West Side Woman's Club, Chicago, 82
Western Negro Press Association, 84
Western University, Kansas, **103**, 103–4
Wetherill, Julie K., 45
"What Is the More Useful Art–Painting or Music?" (Roberts), 123–24
"What of the Children?" (Washington), 62–63
Wheatley, Phillis, 22
White, Albert Blakeslee, 111
Whitman, Alberry A., 23
Whittier, John Greenleaf, 22
Wilberforce University, 7, 19, 33, 48, 67–68, 92, 124
Willard, Frances E., 78
Williams, Andreá N., 7, 8, 14
Williams, Arthur P., 136
Williams, D. B., 125
Williams, Fannie Barrier, 55, 64–65, 68–69
Williams, Heather Andrea, 15, 115
Williams, P. W., 109
Williams, Sylvanie Francoz, 136–38, **137**
Wills, David W., 11, 17, 88
Woman's Christian Temperance Union (WCTU), 55, 56, 66, 76–77; Paris conference (1900), 80

"Woman Suffrage" (Carter), 67–68
"Woman Suffrage" (Dickerson), 57
"Woman's Christian Temperance Union and the Colored Woman, The" (Harper), 45, 76
Woman's Crusade, 76
Woman's Era, The (Black periodical), 42, 76
"Woman's Exalted Station" (Frazier), 46
"Woman's Exalted Station" (Johnson), 57
"Woman's Work and Influence in Home and Church" (Taylor), 59–60
"Women as Educators" (Jones), 120
"Women as Helpers of the Ministers . . ." (Chapelle), 60–61
"Women in Society" (Hubert), 65–66
"Women of Our Race Worthy of Imitation, The" (Bentley), 47–48
"Women of the A.M.E. Church, The" (Upshaw), 49
Women's Aid Circle, 17
women's club movement, 8, 46
Women's Missionary Recorder (AME), 46
Women's Progressive Club, 107
women's roles, 50–51; advocacy for women, 144; and the arts, 52; birth rates for Black women, 128–29; businesswomen, 51; Christianity and treatment of women, 139; church roles, 51, 108, 143; and co-education, 123; contributions to sociology and social work, 55–56; as educators, 118–19; evangelism, 62, 65–66, 108; expanding roles, advocacy for, 106–8; feminism, 57–58; as helpers in church offices, 60–62; in marriage, 59–60; motherhood, 62–63; and philosophical essays, 125; on public transport, 94; "separate spheres," 57–58, 68;

suffrage movement, 67–69; "true womanhood," 57; and use of pseudonyms, 126; World War I, 62. *See also* feminism
Work of the Afro-American Woman, The (G. Mossell), 35, 45
World War I, 62
Wright, R. R., 112

Xenia, Ohio, 67, 130

Yao, Xine, 15
Yates, Josephine Silone, 3, **24**; on French literature, 24–25; "French Literature in the Seventeenth Century," 5; historical essays, 42–43; "Municipal Franchises," 132–33; "Natural Science in the Schools," 125; "Physiology and Hygiene," 125; "River Systems of the United States," 131–32; R. K. Potter pseudonym, 126; "Rural Versus Urban," 133–34
Yates, William W., 42
Yeocum, Ida M., 49
Young People's Missionary and Literary Society, 118
"Young People's Movement, The" (Carter), 111
Young Women's Christian Association, 120
Your Little Brother James (Pemberton), 70

About the Author

COURTESY OF CAITLIN GILMORE

Dr. Cynthia Lee Patterson is associate professor in the English department at the University of South Florida, Tampa campus. She holds a bachelor's degree in English from Miami University, a master's degree in English from Tulane University, and a doctorate in cultural studies from George Mason University. Her interdisciplinary research has received funding from the Smithsonian Institution; the American Antiquarian Society; the Library Company of Philadelphia/Historical Society of Pennsylvania (Andrew W. Mellon Fellowship in African American History); the Winterthur Museum, Garden and Library; the Kentucky Historical Society; and the Pennsylvania State Archives and Museum Commission. Her first book, *Art for the Middle Classes: America's Illustrated Magazines of the 1840s* (University Press of Mississippi, 2010) received an honorable mention in the Research Society for American Periodicals Book Prize for 2010. Her work has appeared in *The Journal of African American History*, *American Periodicals*, *The Journal of American Studies*, *Women's Studies*, *The Southern Quarterly*, *The Pennsylvania Magazine of History and Biography*, and *The Florida Historical Quarterly*, among other periodicals.

Dr. Patterson's research interests include Black print culture, women's history (particularly the histories of women's sewing clubs and literary societies), African American religious history, and the intellectual history of Black women in the United States. She has presented her research at conferences sponsored by the African American Intellectual History Society, the Association for the Study of African American Life and History, the Organization of American Historians, the Modern Language Association, the Berkshire Conference on the History of Women, the National Women's Studies Association, the American Literature Association, C19, and the Society for the Study of American Women Writers. From 2010 to 2018, Dr. Patterson coedited *American Periodicals*, the journal of the Research Society for American Periodicals. She currently serves on the advisory boards for the Research Society for American Periodicals and the Kentucky Historical Society.